Richard Hammond is internationally famous for co-presenting *Top Gear* with Jeremy Clarkson and James May. He has produced and presented insightful documentaries for BBC One, examining the lives of two of his heroes, Sir Stirling Moss and Evel Knievel. He has written a number of bestselling books including *On the Edge*, *As You Do* and *Is It Just Me?*

He is married to Mindy and has two daughters, Izzy and Willow. He shares his garage with an ever-changing collection of motorcycles both vintage and current.

RICHARD HAMMOND

A SHORT HISTORY OF THE

MOTORCYCLE

WEIDENFELD & NICOLSON

A W&N paperback

First published in Great Britain in 2018
by Weidenfeld & Nicolson

1 3 5 7 9 10 8 6 4 2

A CIP catalogue record for this book
is available from the British Library.

ISBN 978 1 4746 0115 3

Typeset by Sarah Jackson

Printed and bound by CPI Group (UK) Ltd, Croydon, CR0 4YY

MIX
Paper from
responsible sources
FSC® C104740

CONTENTS

PROLOGUE

It's expensive, dangerous and people hate you for doing it. But we do it anyway. If bikes are in your blood, then they are in there to stay and maybe this little book can help you cope with and better understand your addiction. If they're not in your blood, then maybe this book can explain what it is about them that leads otherwise sensible, sane people to dress from top to toe in ridiculous outfits and head out to get wet, cold, scared and sometimes dead in the pursuit of their passion.

INTRODUCTION

It's the best idea in the world: simple as that. The motorcycle perfectly enables our deep-rooted desires to travel, to explore, to dominate territory and to return to our cave with a deer slung over our shoulder: or the papers in our backpack. But it also chimes with our evolved need to connect with another creature, to travel the road with it in a perfectly symbiotic relationship based on trust, understanding and mutual goals. Horse – Iron Horse; same thing really; apart from the vet's bills and a fear of carrier bags.

The thing is, horses – the alternative and nearest historical equivalent – are essentially out of control and untrustworthy. A motorcycle, by contrast, is entirely trustworthy and any mistake is, and can only be, your own. Yes, the car hit you, but you really thought it wouldn't pull out in front of you? Yes, the bike highsided mid-corner and threw you up a tree – you've only your throttle hand to blame. No bike has ever gone mad and bucked a rider off because it mistook a crow in a bush for a dragon. But like a horse, a motorcycle is also a great way to show off. Rocking up in town in the 1600s astride a magnificent black Friesian stallion – that's a type of horse with really cool, furry feet and a mane you could lose a goat in – would have had the populace gasping with envy, awe or lust, according to their predilections, principles and position. A bike does the same trick for us: they're cool. They represent power and the mastery of it, the ability to travel fast, to be at the kill first or, better still, at the door of your lover before anyone else. For these reasons bikes have acquired a mythical status in appropriately lightning-fast time. Few people fail to at least have an opinion on motorcycles. You may never have ridden one; you may have been born astride one; but either way, you're likely to have an opinion on them. Love, hate, crave, crash, fear or steal; they mean something to all of us and have evolved to that position in tens of thousands of years' less time than it took for the turkey vulture to invent weeing on its legs to avoid sunburn.

IN THE BEGINNING

There were many distractions available to the man or woman about town and country in the late nineteenth century. For work you could pick up heavy stuff and carry it about for other people, you could further a career in an unheated office wearing fingerless gloves and going blind by candlelight or you might try being a shipping magnate, a gout-riddled politician, an opium addict, a vicious, absinthe-crazed satirist or a wealthy builder of bridges and ships from iron or stone or anything else expensive, heavy and barely workable. In your leisure time, you could collect interesting tropical plants and the new and interesting tropical diseases that arrived on these shores with them, pop down to London and laugh at the mad people in Bedlam, strive to develop a cure for new and interesting tropical diseases using a blacksmith's tongs and a steam hammer, or develop a new and interesting tropical disease itself and die. What you couldn't do, at work or leisure, was ride a motorcycle. And the world was a poorer place for it. The streets were full of rose fertiliser and everything, everyone and everywhere was too far away. Most of all, you couldn't rove about the streets with your mates on small-capacity motor-cycles signalling your power, potency and teenage vigour. You were restricted to rolling an old metal hoop around with a stick and developing rickets. We needed the motorcycle and we needed it now. But, and this is a really massive BUT, built out of stone and iron.

There were two key problems facing the early inventors of the motorcycle in the late 1800s.

1. No one had properly invented the bicycle yet.

2. No one had really invented the motor bit either.

We lacked both the 'motor' and the 'cycle' elements, you see, and someone would have to do something about that pretty fast or people might just wake up one day to peer through the soot-laden fog at the mire in the streets below and realise that everything was entirely crap and they needed some fun in their lives. And then there would be trouble.

So, to work: first, the bicycle.

A hardy and, I suspect, irritatingly flamboyant few paraded around on things like Pierre Michaux's 'velocipede'. Made at his blacksmith's company in Paris, it had pedals, but that's about all it had in common with what we would recognise today as a bicycle. So technically, the 'cycle' part is still not there. But already the burgeoning, burning desire for a motorcycle had overtaken us and, unable to resist the creature's siren call, even in the face of the blindingly obvious fact that it could and would never work, Pierre's son, Ernest, fitted a steam engine to one of his dad's velocipedes. He had created the Michaux-Perreaux steam velocipede which, apart from being a singularly terrible name, was also a singularly poor substitute for a BMW R1000RR HP4 Carbon Edition.

Somehow, despite the obvious futility of pursuing the refinement of a machine that would always be required to lug around its own weight many times over in coal and risked detonating its boiler at any time and levelling the town, factory, leafy suburb or school playground where it was being used, the Americans got involved and Lucius Copeland, himself an American, which was very exotic back then, though it didn't in any way guarantee the possession of a sound head on sensible shoulders, came up with what he declared to be the first 'successful' 'Moto-Cycle'.

Successful, perhaps in terms only he understood, because it was, as you can see, ridiculous and despite his rather optimistic hijacking of something close to the proper name for the thing, the thing itself wasn't quite ready for the streets. Or lanes. Or anywhere but the skip at the back of the factory.

note to above

Americans, though, prided themselves on being a resilient, determined lot, something they had demonstrated only comparatively recently in taking over the continent they called home. And they were not to be put off by something so slight as dismal failure. Besides, inventing stuff was fabulously on-fashion and they persevered with inventing both the motor and the cycle. Pierre Lallement – yes, that's a French name, because he was an employee of Pierre Michaux, the French blacksmith who founded the first company to produce the velocipede – claimed to have had a hand in developing the prototype for the machine and filed the first bicycle patent with the US Patent Office in 1866. Sylvester Roper then developed

DIED IN THE SADDLE.

Sylvester H. Roper Was Riding a Steam-Propelled Bicycle.

Had Made Fast Time on Charles River Park When He Suddenly Fell—Had Shut Off the Steam as If on Premonition of the End.

SYLVESTER H. ROPER AND HIS FATAL INVENTION.

Poor old Sylvester died while riding one of his later steam bikes at a bicycle race in 1896. While doing a demonstration run at over 40mph his face apparently turned grey and he wobbled to a stop and fell off. He'd had a heart attack. Probably due to overexcitement.

Opposite: This dapper chap is Lucius Copeland, inventor of the contraption that he's proudly standing beside. This 1884 single-cylinder steam powered machine looked like a penny-farthing with an engine but unlike the former it's the front wheel that steers. No doubt absolutely terrifying at its 15mph top speed.

a twin-cylinder steam velocipede with a coal-fired boiler. It wasn't very good but he stuck with it, being an American and all, and by 1894 he had developed a new version. Sadly, he died of a heart attack while demonstrating it in Cambridge, Massachusetts in 1896. Shame really – well, obviously it's a shame, people sad etc. – but he had invented by then what many people consider to be the first motorcycle. And the most significant thing about it? Well it wasn't the motor, which was still an impractical, wheezy steam engine, but the bicycle bit … that's where the secret to success lay and why there are those who credit Roper with being the inventor of, if not THE, then ONE of THE first motorcycles.

Roper's 1896 bike was based on the then super-modern safety bicycle. And that is big news and a sign that the stars were lining up for everything to come together and make the moment perfect for the invention of the most important, exciting, trouser-tweakingly wonderful invention of them all, the modern motorcycle.

Up until about 1885, bicycle riders had been limited to machines with a front wheel bigger than the London Eye and a rear wheel off a piano. They were hilariously, horribly

dangerous and only existed because no one had really thought up gearing. The front wheel was so huge because, as I am sure you are aware, every rotation of the pedals, fixed to the centre of that huge front wheel, resulted in a rotation of the wheel itself. The circle turned by the pedals was small, only as large as could be articulated by the feet and legs of the man or woman pedalling. But when translated to the massive outer rim of the big wheel itself, that one rotation added up to a much, much bigger distance than that travelled by the rider's feet. The outside circumference of the big wheel was going a lot faster and a lot further than the smaller circumference described by the pedals. And then you hit a low wall, swung over the front wheel and were catapulted head first into a coal shed.

By 1885 that fad had ended at last with the introduction of gearing; a bicycle was invented on which the chain-wheel was roughly twice the size of the rear sprocket, achieving the same gear ratio as the penny-farthing's without the need to travel to the shops on something tall enough to pitch you into the next county when you fell off. So, it had two spoked wheels of equal size, a chain-driven rear wheel and direct steering. The English inventor who formalised the design of the 'safety bicycle' was industrialist John Kemp Starley. In fact, the name 'safety bicycle' had been coined a little earlier to attach to the creation of another English inventor, Harry John Lawson, in 1876. But his invention, unlike Starley's, didn't have the benefit of gearing, and that was the key development that made the thing functional. Neither did it have the benefit of the added title, 'Rover'; another little creation of Starley's, when he called his bike the 'Rover Safety Bicycle', which is a bit boring. I'd

Compare a penny-farthing to the Rover and Cogent bicycles advertised above
and the words safety bicycle need little explanation. Which would you rather
fall off?

have called it the 'Rotational Thrust Warp Machine' or the
'Compact Cyclical Strike Urge Warrior'. But it was OK, because
it was the bicycle that served as the basis of Roper's machine
and anyway, within a year of its launch, Gottlieb Daimler had
strapped an internal combustion engine to it to create the
Reitwagen and in doing so had invented the first motorcycle
– or the other ONE of THE first motorcycles. But let's not get
caught up in who invented THE first and who invented ONE of
THE first whatever, let's just agree that by 1896 everything was
looking rosy, fast and a little bit more dangerous from then on.

Before we move on, I want to make sure that we're not
getting carried away here. The first motorcycles were pretty

terrible. They were slow, unreliable, leaky and difficult to steer and stop. So quite dangerous then. But context is everything; and most things were terrible or dangerous or a combination of both back then. If your washing was dried in a mangle, you would be impressed in 1895 by a motorcycle with a De Dion-Bouton engine generating a monumental half a horsepower. Especially if you had ridden to work on one of Daimler's earliest bicycles with its wooden frame and wooden spoked wheels with iron rims.

Then there was a lot of refinement and tweaking of this and that, to the point where, by the 1900s, motorcycles made by the fledgling Indian company were producing an unimaginable 1.75 horsepower and propelling their brave owners to speeds of 25 miles an hour.

HERE TO STAY

We are twentieth-century bikers. Out of the goddam way, please madam ...

While there are those things that take a while to catch on – democracy, monogamy, hygiene and such – motorcycling was not one of them. As the smog-laden, rickety 1800s rolled round into the optimistic, thrillingly new though still smoggy and rickety 1900s, the motorcycle had caught on, big time. The first motorcycle magazine called, imaginatively enough, *Motor Cycling*, was launched in 1902. And people cared about this. In response to the warm reception that it had immediately received, the magazine dedicated a page to reflecting on how wonderful it was and how much everybody loved it. On this page we can read about J.A. Lewis of Ipswich who wrote, following receipt of his copy of the new magazine, to declare, 'Undoubtedly a good value for one penny; was pleased with it', and what finer praise could there be? Well there was more: C.G. Shore of Croydon must have been wrestling with his Englishman's stiff upper lip as might a picnicker with his tablecloth on a windy day when

These splendid gentleman are obviously admiring this 1903 'experimental' Matchless, glad that they're not sitting in the thing on the back. The single-seat trailer idea didn't catch on.

he wrote to say, 'Really a magnificent and instructive paper.' He even added, at the risk of being banished from English society for the crime of rabid sentimentality, with sinister undertones of something like publicly expressed happiness, 'I wish it every success.' This was 1902, barely six years after Roper and/or Daimler had combined Starley and/or Lawson's safety bicycle design with a proper, if rudimentary, internal combustion engine to create the first motorcycles. The motorcycle was still blinking to open its eyes for the first time, standing on wobbly legs and looking for its mother's dangling teat, yet it was thrust into the limelight like a Beatle stepping off an aeroplane some sixty years later. *Motor Cycling* magazine included quotes from 'The Trade' too. What trade? How can there have been a trade for something so new? You may as well talk of a baby's body of work or a kitten's Facebook account – actually, there are millions of those,

'Crikey Cuthbert, that shop next to the butcher in the high street has got the new Regina and it's £45.' It's 1902 and the motor bicycle is catching on.

but you'll take my point. Nevertheless, under 'What the Trade Says', we read that the Enfield Cycle Co. Ltd declared, 'Have received No. 1 of *Motor Cycling* on which I hasten to congratulate you.'

Strettons Ltd of Cheltenham wrote, 'Congratulate you upon the first issue of *Motor Cycling*. It quite fulfils our expectations, and we feel sure it will be the recognised organ of the motor cycle trade just as *Cycling* is of the Cycle trade.'

Perhaps most telling of all is another section on *Motor Cycling's* page of shameless self-adoration. Under 'What the Press Says' are quotes from the *Daily Mail*, the *Pall Mall Gazette*, the Birmingham *Midland Express* and others. These are mainstream newspapers reporting on a specialist magazine launched to inform those taking part in a new and, to most eyes, frankly peculiar pastime. That the new pastime warrants coverage in the mainstream press at all suggests there was a large groundswell of interest already building.

The *Daily Express*, we are told, 'considers the pastime established' and writes joyfully that:

Motorcyclists now have a paper to themselves. The first number of Motor Cycling, *an off-shoot of that excellent weekly* Cycling, *has just been published. From the quantity of news and illustrations to say nothing of the advertisements, it is evident that the new pastime already stands high in popular favour.*

Girl bikers aren't a new thing. This American couple are about to take their his 'n' hers machines out for a ride. Her safety headgear looks the most convincing.

Don't you just completely love it when something catches on quickly and sweeps across nations to consume our passions and thoughts? Not disease and stuff, obviously, or fake religions or weird convictions, but when it's something good and wholesome and useful, like skateboards and hula hoops in the generations to follow. In this instance, I think it's plain to see that the motorcycle caught on so quickly because it was, in the collective consciousness, already with us. For the motorcycle to exist we first needed the motor and the cycle. By 1900 we had them and they were almost immediately combined to match up to an idea that was already in our heads. It is as though we already knew about the Ducati 1299 Panigale S as a destination and were just setting out merrily to get there as quickly as possible. In talking about the new magazine for this entirely new breed, the Birmingham *Midland Express* 'doubts not its value' and has, clearly, a sense that these are the early stages of something exciting and important when it writes, 'If the quality of the letterpress and illustrations evidenced by the first number can be maintained, *Motor Cycling* will become popular, and will unquestionably prove of value to the followers of this important phase of cycling.'

THE BIKER ARRIVES

Something else to take from the early press coverage regarding the motorcycle and motorcycling: it seems to have been driven not only by those already tinkering with early automobiles but also, and perhaps more fervently, by the cycling fraternity. The magazine *Motor Cycling* was, as the *Daily Express* reminded us, an offshoot of *Cycling*, a weekly magazine aimed at those who had taken up the still new pastime of riding about on the newly-invented safety bicycle both as a pastime and as transport. Far from decrying this new and noisy relative of their chosen steed, cyclists embraced it as a long-lost friend. I don't wish to be cynical but – which means I do wish to be cynical, much like when a taxi driver opens with, 'I don't want to be racist but …' – anyway, my question, despite the obvious cynicism is, would the motorcycle or its equivalent be met with such enthusiasm today by what could be seen as the 'old guard', enthusiasts of something clearly about to be replaced by this newer, better alternative? I doubt it. But cyclists, by and large, seem to have taken one look at the motorcycle and decided, 'Yup, that's the thing for me'.

Take, as an example, well-known cyclist of the time and prolific author on the subject, Mr G. Lacy Hillier. His approach to the things is pragmatic, to say the very least. In an article headed 'The Motor Bicycle, Has it Come to Stay?', printed in *Motor Cycling* in March 1902, he makes it pretty clear that he won't be protesting the arrival of the new machine in any way.

'Bicycle riding has been a pastime for some 30 to 35 years, steadily increasing in popular favour and happily emancipated from the cad-on-castors slur of some years ago.'

Oh good, people are already deciding that bikers, even Victorian ones with massive moustaches and silly trousers pedalling bicycles, are a bit bad-ass.

'The cycle is now recognised as a convenient means of locomotion by all classes.'

Note: he doesn't talk about Lycra-clad congestion enthusiasts kicking the flanks of other people's pride and joy because they had the temerity to take it out on the roads for the maintenance of which they pay a very great deal of tax. In fact, there's a hint here that the bicycle was already being seen not as a novelty item but as a means of transport for the masses. Something that G. Lacy Hillier addresses head on:

On the point of cost – The motor bicycle is, of course, much more within reach than a car; in fact, compared with the ordinary safety the motor-bicycle is already cheap, the results of keen competition in the cycle trade, thus benefiting the users of the new vehicle.

As to storage or stabling [Note: I cannot describe the visceral thrill that pulses through me when I read the word 'stabling' in this context. It immediately connects with the subtle, underlying sensation that a bike is alive, a creature with which to share the road and the adventures it holds.] – The motor-bicycle scores heavily. Many cyclists, especially suburban residents, cannot stable even an ordinary tricycle, but the motor-bicycle is as easily stabled as a safety and, to this point alone assures the motor-bicycle a large amount of popularity. Stabling-out involves expense as well as the possibility of the machines being interfered with._

Four smiling chaps pose with a Triumph 500 Model H in 1914. Ironically this is the bike the War Department chose for despatch riding duties. How many of these men survived the First World War?

Oh good, we're getting precious about our steeds now. And not, I suspect, just on account of the cost. Shades perhaps of the Hells Angels' dreadful future punishments for any thieving tike tempted to interfere even the tiniest bit with the badged bike of a patch-bearing member of their clan. It only takes one failed bike thief waking up to find himself tied to a chair at the back of a warehouse surrounded by bearded men in leather jackets holding large spanners in a fashion that suggests the thing they're about to go to work on with them is not a bolt, to spread and intensify the concept of a magical bond between man – or semi-homicidal maniac – and machine and thus elevate that machine to mythical status.

G. Lacy Hillier goes on to talk about how the motorcycle, 'in a classic phrase, fills a long felt want', and proposes that it will find its own field and retain it, that cycle-making firms with a reputation for sound work will find that it brings grist to the mill, that it will induce many riders to take an interest in the sport, and bring in many new men – in short, that it has come at just the right juncture, when the trade outlook is improving and enterprise reviving.

And in another piece of foresight, when he says,

The speed generally will be faster than that of ordinary cycling, with a correspondingly exhilarating effect, and there is much to interest the rider in the skilful management of his mount. Thus I expect to see many a rider long missed from the haunts where cyclists most do congregate once more frequenting them …

it is as though he has just returned from a blast up the Cat and Fiddle pass on a Kawasaki H2 and a bacon sarnie in a car park with all his biker mates. We were already bikers; we just needed the bikes.

Right, we've got our bikes. Now what do we do with them?

FIRST MOTORCYCLE SHOW

My entire childhood was spent looking at motorcycles. Nothing else. By the age of ten or eleven I could spot a bike from the car window and reel off its name, manufacturer, stats pertaining to the engine capacity and any specialist purpose or talents of the machine. No one was interested, but I would reel them off all the same. Looking at bikes and, better still, being among them, roaming through a group of them as you might stumble across a herd of grazing antelope on an African savannah is almost, but never quite, as much fun as riding them. A fact realised very quickly by the buying public and, more importantly, by the selling trade very shortly after the motorcycle's eventual arrival. A few short years after the first examples of the breed had floundered to their wheels and taken to the roads came the first motorcycle show. Technically, it was a bit of an invasion of an existing event, but the pioneer bikers took to it as their own when it first cropped up on the social calendar at the Crystal Palace Motor Show on 14–22 February 1902. Given that it was still very much a fledgling creation, it might be expected that there would be only a couple of newfangled motorcycles in a corner of the exhibition, but it sounds, from the articles in *Motor Cycle* and the press at the time, rather as though the two-wheelers invaded the four-wheelers' event. They certainly caught the public imagination.

> *For the first time, we believe, in England, a special motor cycle section has been arranged, and this promises to be one of the most interesting and representative collections under one roof ever seen. Here the well-known Ariel, Excelsior, Minerva, Quadrant, Mitchell, Derby, Chapelle, New Hudson, Phoenix, Humber, Werner and new-type Werner and several other types will be on view, and on trial for the most part, in the grounds.*

Bikes have always been a good way to impress the girls and this young man is on the case as he proudly stands by his 1911 Minerva 3.5hp.

Hold on, the things have only just been invented and there's a list of manufacturers as long as a policeman's extended arm. The internet revolution then is not, by a long way, the first example of human ingenuity and entrepreneurial drive spotting an opportunity and really rolling up its sleeves to make sure it wasn't missed.

The show gave visitors the chance to watch motorcycles and cars being ridden and driven and even to have a crack at operating the machines themselves. On Wednesday 19 February, a J. van Hooydonk, probably inspired to feats of derring-do and bravery in order to live up to his heroic and magnificent name, was advertised as setting out on a 200-mile non-stop trial at the Crystal Palace track on his Phoenix bicycle.

WHERE THE BIKE IS NOW

We've spoken about the history of the motorcycle and how it was basically the realisation of something that we knew all along we wanted. No sooner were the motor and cycle elements invented than they were combined to create the machine that had stalked our dreams since caveman times. And no sooner had the machine been born than mankind set about racing it and fighting with it. But let's take a moment to remind ourselves that these were indeed the early days of the motorcycle and, while promising, it wasn't quite there yet. This is how a motorcycle of the early 1900s worked and how the rider operated it. Be warned: if you passed your motorcycle test last week, you may struggle to recognise some of this as the same thing. In any way.

And there are early signs that we are, perhaps, starting to sort out how the machines should actually be operated. By 1902 manufacturers and riders alike are aware of the pre-requisites for any machine calling itself a motorcycle; number of wheels, an engine and so on. And they have worked out some of the finer points, too: the engine needs to be fed with petrol and air that have been mixed together in the right quantities, it needs to be lubricated with oil to stop the fast-spinning metal parts inside welding themselves together, there needs to be some means of delivering the power made from the engine's hungry consumption of the fuel to the driven wheel and some means of feeding that power in gradually so as to make it possible to pull away smoothly. As a nice touch and a nod to people's finer sensibilities, it might be advantageous to fit the motorcycle also with some means of stopping. But how all these various tasks were carried out and, more particularly, the means by which those various processes were controlled, was still far from standardised. In an article in *The Motor Cycle* about the first bike show at Crystal Palace there is a passage advising visitors to inspect for themselves 'a decided novelty, which the Quadrant Co. will show for the first time'. It transpires that the reason they have given the Quadrant Co.'s display such a fervent nod is wrapped up in the business of trying to make these new machines usable.

> *The Quadrant motor bicycle is fitted with the Minerva engine and it is in the working of it that the main improvements we have alluded to will be found. One lever does the work of four — that will sum up the whole thing — and simplicity is gained at one stroke. This lever controls the switch, the gas supply, the sparking and the exhaust. Those who have done any traffic riding on a motor will quickly grasp, metaphorically speaking, the great boon which the above will confer upon the motor bicyclist.*

Well yes. Given that the rider seemed to be responsible for

each and every aspect and element of their 'steed's' operation, right down to the sparking at the spark plug and the mixing of the combustible combination of petrol and air being fed into the confines of the chamber, it would seem that while offering all the excitement a modern-day motorcycle can bring, these early machines were fit to be operated only by an octopus with an engineering degree and absolutely no fear whatsoever.

CAMARADERIE

Something that matters a great deal to the modern biker is the existence of biking camaraderie. This is not some imagined notion dreamed up in a soppy west London media 'break out space' or the hopeful imaginings of some teenage idealist, it is a true and real thing. Ride a bike anywhere and you will, at some point, encounter another. And in nine times out of ten that other biker shall return your cheery, helmeted nod. These nods are, in themselves, more complex, more nuanced and more loaded with meaning than might be apparent to the non-biker. Should the weather be bad – and yes, it generally is when you're on a bike – then the nod will be slighter in distance but slightly elongated in duration, the better to communicate a sense of shared endurance, of being the only two out of the otherwise cocooned drivers in their dreary cars, who are prepared to suffer discomfort and increased danger in order to pursue and stick with their chosen means of transport. If it's a bright, clear day – it won't be, whatever the man or woman on the telly said and however it was looking when you set off – then the nod will be crisp and brief but with plenty

'I think it could be your piffle valve, madam.' Roadside help from an unemployed ex-artillery officer who's set up an al fresco repair business outside Sevenoaks.

of articulation of the neck; an altogether bouncier and briefer acknowledgement that says, in its one, simple dip, 'Hello mate, not got time to hang around but damn, isn't this just the best thing in the world.'

Likewise, on encountering a fellow rider standing at the side of the road, his machine perhaps in a hedge or propped on its stand leaking essential fluids, most bikers will stop and check that all is well or if disaster has struck. Now this last point requires brief clarification: it is not, sadly, as common as one might hope. It was common, extremely so, as late as the seventies and eighties and into the early nineties. In those decades, bikes were still prone to mechanical failures and bike kit prone to leaking wind and water, rendering the poor biker incapable of riding safely, both of which circumstances necessitated the occasional roadside halt. Bikers would always stop on seeing a fellow brother or sister of the road in trouble, because the next time it might well be them in need of assistance, company or sympathy. Things have changed, though; bikes are endlessly reliable and clothing is permanently impervious to the weather, meaning any biker stopped at the side of the road is pulling over for a quiet pee or to take a picture on their phone. It might also be that bikers themselves have changed, have become fundamentally different in the twenty-first century, but that is an issue for later in this book. For now, let me simply establish that biking brings brotherhood, fraternity and camaraderie and, it seems, has done so right from the very start.

CONKING OUT

Perhaps it was the complexity of operating an early motorcycle and the feeling of smugness that must come from mastering such a thing that led to a very early sense of camaraderie among motor bicyclists. If you had spent your every waking hour working out how to operate a thing and then, when out on it saw another coming the other way, you would be more than happy to stop and exchange views and experiences. Assuming, that is, you could stop, given that most bikes had a rim brake at the front, if any, and possibly a back pedalling-operated brake at the back. Not only that, but the sudden evolution of a social circle around the motorcycle meant you could generally be assured of help from a passing biker should your machine run into mechanical trouble, which it absolutely, definitely would, at some point very shortly after setting off.

Here, a contributor to *Motor Cycling* writes in to an early edition to share his experiences of breakdowns – of which he seems to have had a great many – and inadvertently shows us how the biking fraternity was already binding itself tight together.

...The next rider I met in trouble was on the Maidstone
Road – he was going to Folkestone, had got as far
as Wrotham and then stopped. Upon examination
I discovered he had run the old oil out of his crank chamber
and not replaced the screw. I had to substitute this with a
pin of wood.

Later on in his lengthy letter listing just some of the many disasters that he reports have befallen him and other bikers he has met in his travels, our brave roadside knight recalls finding yet another rider in trouble – I rather suspect they were actually all in trouble, all of the time, and going out on an early bike ride was to set out only to see which particular emergencies would be waiting on the road to greet them that day.

On another occasion I met a friend pedalling his motor
bicycle and found his batteries were run down, so obtained
some electric bell wire [of course you did, the stuff is
everywhere] and coupled his coil to my accumulator
(which is a Peto and Radford) and we came home together
off the one accumulator, but I found riding side-by-side
very tricky, and every time we got a bit wide the wires
parted.

Well yes, hooking your bike up to another and riding home tied together with a bit of bell wire – whatever bell wire is, I want some – would be, I should imagine, both tricky and really quite dangerous. And yet he survived to write in to a magazine and share his story. Bikers were already, it seems, a cut above the rest and showing early on their promise to improve themselves and be worthy of their wondrous new machines.

PREVENTING CONKING OUT

Proper Prior Preparation Prevents ... you know the rest.

Any activity worth engaging in involves some preparation. Be it splashing on the cologne before a night out, sharpening a carving knife, packing a suitcase or waterproofing a walking boot – I am aware, yes, that some of these examples may apply to my life rather than yours, but we all have our equivalents – anything you are going to do that will grab and hold your attention properly will require a bit of setting up. A spot of preparation. Early biking required, it would seem, a lot of it.

In order to be ready for whatever mechanical crisis arrived on a trip out on your early motorcycle – and arrive, it surely would – riders were advised to carry a few tools and spares with them. Quite a few: so many, in fact, that it's remarkable today that bikes didn't naturally evolve to be bigger than buses. Here is what *Motor Cycling* magazine, in a supplement 'Roadside Repairs and how to Effect Them', advised that you pop in your saddlebag before setting out:

1. A good, adjustable spanner; see that this opens out to the size of the largest nut on the motor [Hmm, seems to me that this would mean finding one as big as your head]
2. A pair of light 'combination' pliers having wire cutters and tube or nut grip
3. A small but strong screwdriver, with the blade well tempered – broad and sharp
4. A small oil can and larger oil can for lubricating oil
5. A small flat (medium cut) file
6. A very small dead-smooth half round and flat file
7. A yard of No.16 copper wire
8. 2ft of asbestos string
9. A few inches of $1/16$ inch thick asbestos sheet
10. A foot of rubber 'insulating' strip ½ inch wide
11. A small piece of marine glue
12. A good tyre repairing outfit
13. A strip of pliable leather ¼ inch thick.

It would be unwise to be caught today with some of these things about your person, lest the assumption is made that you are a bomb-maker, a fetishist or a mad hoarder. Either way you are going to end up on television quite soon and will not be cast in a good light. The list goes on.

Also remember it is advisable to obtain these duplicate fittings:
One spare sparking plug,
one spare exhaust valve with its spring and collar,
one trembler blade and platinum-tipped screw,

one washer for exhaust cover,
one extra belt fastener,
a few spare nuts for the various jointed rods
and a small spare 4-volt battery.

A puncture repair kit this is not. Although the writer does advise us that 'The above list may seem a very long one but really the things take up very little room and all except the last will easily go in a square valise 7 inches wide by 4 inches high by 2 inches deep.'

Really? I want this guy to come and sort my loft.

You don't need to be an engineer to appreciate that anyone setting out with such an arsenal of tools and materials is prepared to get stuck into any task up to and including rebuilding the machine from base metals mined and refined by the side of the road if necessary. These are not referred to as the 'pioneer' years without good reason. Had the kit we are advised to carry included a bow and arrow and a buffalo hide they would not have stood out as unusual among the rest.

GOING PLACES

Time to travel. And it will take time.

Given that you might, at any moment, have to pull over and establish a rubber plantation to enable you to eventually tap the trees for enough rubber to replace a snapped belt, people's attitude towards travelling by anything driven by a motor was as unfathomably different to ours today as was a Victorian draping a veil over a piano leg lest it excited a visiting male into a frenzy of barely-containable lust and he disgraced himself with a sideboard. Motorists on two, four and even three wheels set out with every intention of using their new machines as transport. They didn't always leave the house simply seeking to uncover disaster and deal with it manfully by the side of the road; sometimes they actually wanted to get somewhere. The buying public had really taken up the idea that motorcycles and cars were for getting to places too distant to reach by horse or on foot. And they were incredibly forgiving of the fact that no manufacturer seemed able, by the beginning of the 1900s, to supply them with a machine that could in any way whatsoever be relied upon other than to break down immediately and deposit them by the side of the road to be laughed at, presumably, by the many doubters who could have occupied entire fun-filled weekends wandering the highways and byways to snigger at crestfallen rich people sitting in a patch of oily mud and wondering how to cover the eighty miles back home without the advantage of the swanky machine that had so willingly transported them eighty miles away from it before expiring in a cloud of steam, smoke and humiliation. As a source of entertainment, for both motorist and doubter alike, the roads must have been an unbeatable and seemingly unlimited resource in 1902.

The attitude of mind required by early road users for a spot of motoring in the early 1900s must be borne in mind when we consider from this distance of time the machines

Carl Stearns Clancy before and after his round the world ride. Setting off on his new four-cylinder Henderson in 1912, Clancy arrived back home a year later having made the first circumnavigation of the globe by motorcycle. Back then it really was a long way round.

available to them. Or rather, that the attitude of mind was necessitated by those very machines. While we look at them today as antiques, preserved in museums or leaking oil on our own garage floor, they really were used to get around the place and people, somehow, travelled huge distances on what are today seen by some as fragile ornaments.

In July 1902 a Mr Ernest H. Arnott wrote to *Motor Cycling* magazine about his trip from Land's End to John O'Groats on a Werner motorcycle. The magazine states quite plainly that they are keen to print his story for the positive PR it brings, 'believing that performances of this kind accomplished on standard machines as offered to the public are of the greatest value, showing as they do the capabilities of the motor-bicycle for practical purposes'. Well, yes, and no. It worked, he did it, he got there and it would have taken longer to walk. A bit longer. It took him 2 days and 17 hours to complete the 888 miles. He spent a backside-numbing 47 hours and 55 minutes in the saddle to do it and never left his hotel of a morning later than 3 a.m. or arrived for the evening before 7.30 p.m. It was, naturally, not a journey without adventure and surprise. He encountered a stray mule in Land's End on setting off, got lost after Redruth, complained about the hideous state of the roads around Wigan and the weather in the Lake District and commented on the road over the hills through Dalwhinnie and Kingussie, 'I suppose it was intended for a road once, but it now resembles a grass plot with loads of loose flints and stones laid over it.' He seems to have suffered only one puncture – and this in an age when one might reasonably expect a stroll across the kitchen to be interrupted by at least one or more – and to have tackled the hills and gradients in fine style. Having said that, a chap in 1902 would have borne adversity with the stiffest of upper lips and so cannot be expected to comment that any encounter on the right side of being subjected to a concerted attack by a pride of lions or roasted on a spit was anything other than perfectly pleasant. Nevertheless, this brave adventurer made it. And there were others who ventured further afield. Bikers toured Europe, competed in the fearsome Paris to Vienna race, wandered the globe, or as far as the south of France, anyway, and made it back alive to share with the waiting world their tales of adventure.

But such adventures were not always easy. In fact no, they were never easy. Operating a motorcycle in the early 1900s can be compared with riding a modern motorcycle only if you were to try operating a Victorian printing press at the same time. And had, before setting off, removed several critical engine components and disconnected the brakes. And so it demanded the correct attitude of mind; an awareness that things might break down, that the journey might be extended by a number of hours or days and that you would, probably, get there in the end and may as well make the best of it. In a piece that seems to look largely at the troubling issue of what to wear while motorcycling – something we shall address in more detail elsewhere in this book – a keen cyclist in what he describes as the 'Transition Stage' to becoming a motorcyclist describes his efforts to keep warm on a motor bicycle. Something made harder, he believes, by the comparative lack of exercise when travelling under power as opposed to pedalling a heavy bicycle about the place.

*Where the Motorcycle differs in this matter from the cycle
is in this respect. If one gets at all cold when on the cycle,
a hard steady plug will quickly restore the circulation,
and even on a cold winter's day, and when clad in a
costume suited to the exercise, one can reach home with
the body gently aglow. Whilst, if the weather be broiling
hot, one can take it steadily where pedalling is necessary
and by free-wheeling on every opportunity, a fair rate of
progression can be attained without distress and a cool
siesta under a tree is yet another ally in the battle with the
heat.*

Yes, of course. The roads are often littered with people
opting to interrupt their journey with a siesta under some
trees. This, then, was the attitude brought to the newly
emerging motorcyling by those making the 'transition' from
cycling. If you are prepared to stop and sleep the afternoon
away under a tree because you got a bit warm cycling to the
next town, you're not going to take it as badly as might we
modern motorists if you have to stop for a minute to fix an
ailing valve on your motorcycle. The pioneer motorcyclist of
1902 was completely suited, then, to the pioneer motorcycle.
The scene was set, the need answered and things could only
get steadily better for the newly born biker.

By 1914, the motorcycle was established not as a plaything
but as a serious means of transport. It was cheap and, well, it
was cheap. And ready to go to war …

LET'S GO RACING

Great, we've got our unicorn. Now what are we going to do with it?

Well, there were two options:

Option 1: Race it

Give a couple of chaps – and yes, it does seem to be an affliction peculiar to chaps perhaps more than women – anything at all, from a kitchen chair to a new lawnmower, leave them alone with their new things and on your return you will find said chaps racing them. You just will.

A cleverer man than me – and there are, I accept, many such – might be able to explain just why this is; where this seemingly primal urge to pitch one thing against another comes from. But whatever the source of this urgent compulsion, the fact remains that it is there and time and time again throughout history we have seen it surge forwards with us clutched in its fiery grasp. Many have died and, sadly, continue to do so in the business of proving that thing A is faster than

An unknown rider poses for the camera before taking part in the Crystal Palace road races in September 1927. He looks pretty cramped on the bike with his bum barely off the ground.

thing B around place C. Whether the things be evenly matched and have been developed specifically for racing or for making toast seems not to deter the caveman racer in us all and whether the place chosen for their race is likewise custom built for the purpose or a kitchen floor matters not a jot. And so it was inevitable that seemingly only minutes after the first approximation of a motorcycle wheezed out of the shed, someone built another and pitched it against the first in a race.

The first bike race

The first official race in the UK, and boy is this ever one of those matters subject to debate and pub-ranting, took place

Riders crest a rise at Crystal Palace. The London venue, used for car and motorcycle racing into the early 1970s, held the first motorcycle races in Great Britain, in 1902.

in 1902 at the Crystal Palace. The motorcycle by then, let us remind ourselves, was still in foetal form. The bicycle upon which the machine was based had only been invented within the preceding couple of decades and the motor element of it likewise was barely an infant. And yet on Saturday 15 February 1902, on what was reported to be an unexpectedly bright and 'genial' day, competitors and 'a large gathering of spectators' gathered, we are told in the February 1902 edition of *The Motor Cycle*, to witness the first race meeting in England confined to purely motor bicycles. Many cyclists of note and otherwise were there to celebrate the inception of the new sport and (incidentally) to pick up tips that would guide them in the choice of motor machine.

Shades already, perhaps, of the commercially minded spotting the opportunity offered by a large gathering of people with a shared interest in something that could be sold to them by the canny operator. And the cynic in one might prompt a few further observations concerning this first and formative gathering in the name of motorcycle racing. Aside from the immediate and inevitable interest from the commercial operators, there were several other familiarly contemporary themes equally quick to find form in this first meeting.

Rules: We love a rulebook

Another thing a group of chaps will do when left together with any implement, machine or moveable object, aside from race it, is argue about the rules governing the race. Often this argument will, in fact, occupy all of the time available for the actual race and at the expiration of said time the competitors will find themselves in possession of a set of rules hewn from the very blood, sweat and tears of those present but with no actual racing experience from which to gauge the appropriateness or otherwise of those rules. And straightaway, by 15 February 1902, the pub bores had already got hold of the thing and, sure enough, embarked upon lengthy and I should imagine impossibly dreary debate concerning the formation of officially recognised rules and regulations. God but blokes are predictable. We really are.

This was the debut event for the newly formed Motor Cycling Club who had turned up, no doubt, bearing with them an appropriately weighty tome detailing the many rules and regulations that their town hall deliberations had delivered.

But this was new; the whole idea of meeting to race motor-cycles had never happened on this scale before. And sure enough, confusion seems to have reigned. For a start, there were a lot of different classes and disciplines for a sport still barely off the delivery room weighing scales.

There were three races planned for the track and then the whole event would move on in the afternoon to the grounds of the Palace where there would be further hill climbs and speed trials. The morning's track events were broken down according to horsepower into four classes, peaking with those packing a mighty 'more than 2hp'. In the first event, the riders took off in two heats with the eventual winner, a Mr Tessier, covering the five miles of the final in 9 minutes and 2.5 seconds.

Things got a bit more complicated in the second event, in which all riders took off in one heat. Admittedly there were only four of them, but nevertheless this was, I should imagine, quite a moment to behold for the spectators.

For the sake of preserving this momentous occasion, we should name the riders. They were (and I would like you to hum 'Born to Be Wild' while reading the names):

H.W. Stones on a Rex 1¾hp

L.S. Watson on a Chapelle 1¾hp

J.H. Dickinson on a J.D. 1¾hp

E.T. Arnott on a Princeps 1¾hp.

None of them benefited from racing leathers, a hydration consultant or the attentions of pit lane girls, but they should all be remembered as true pioneers of the very same sport that today has young men and women gazing with itchy fingers at modern motorcycle racing's exotic machinery, sinuous tracks and tight leather trousers, according to their proclivities.

The day didn't go entirely well. In the contemporary report, *The Motor Cycle* tells us that in the first event, 'Watson adopted a funny position and lost interest before the finish.' Not something on which modern bookmakers regularly give odds today. Stones led on his Rex, ahead of the Princeps until it had to stop. The Rex, we read, 'finished solus'; so I can only imagine that the rider of the J.D., Mr Dickinson, was distracted by a shop or stopped for tea. Congratulations all the same to H.W. Stones on his Rex, who completed the five-mile race in 9 minutes and 40 seconds, making a blistering average of 31mph. After the track events, the racing moved to the grounds for hill-climbing and speed contests on a track measuring three-quarters of a mile, running from the road to the terrace, where further confusion over the rules resulted in disqualifications that, together with punctures and snapped belts, ended some riders' dreams early and gave others an advantage they hadn't expected.

As surprising as the complexity of the class distinctions between what was, after all, only a tiny range of motor cycles, was the complexity of the rules governing the racing itself. And it befuddled some riders.

The novelty of racing on the track naturally created some slight confusion amongst the competitors, one or two having to be disqualified for a breach of the rules forbidding the pushing off to cross the starting line with both feet.

Oh God, the rule-makers really had sat down at a table and thrashed this one out over brown beer and brown food, hadn't they? How galling then to discover, on the day, that the eager competitors in this new sport had paid rather more attention to fiddling the scrutineering than reading the bit in the rules about 'pushing off to cross the starting line with both feet'. Questions arose, we are told, 'as to the genuineness of the declaration of anent horsepower; but the rules were laid down explicitly enough and the matter can be safely left in the hands of the club'. Brilliant: so riders were already playing the odds and trying to squeeze any advantage they could. Given that the classes covered a pretty narrow bandwidth of differences (see below), the advantages gained by fibbing to the officials about the output of your mighty machine must have been slight, but every second counted right from the start.

Classes at the first race:

Motors catalogued at 1½hp or under

Motors not more than 1½hp

Motors not exceeding 2hp

Motors at more than 2hp.

But some of those breaking the rules were exposed and, whether their sins resulted from criminal intent or unreliable paperwork, they were duly disqualified.

I don't imagine that the racers of 1902 were inclined to the same displays of indignant fury and petulant rage as sportsmen and women of today, perhaps due to the calming effect of a cloth cap and a tweed jacket, but I like to picture, nevertheless, scenes of chaos and confusion as those with the rule books patiently explained the rules again and then again to those without the rule book but with the motorcycles.

THE FIRST MOTORCYCLE YOBBOS?

While the competitors no doubt stiffened their upper lips behind their bushy moustaches and dealt manfully with the accusations of being in breach of the rules, there were other elements of this first race meet that bore witness, perhaps, to a more comfortingly mischievous and rebellious streak already forming in the spectators. There were, it seems, an unusual number, perhaps even a suspicious number, of nails found on the track. This was reported in *The Motor Cycle*:

> *A serious complaint arose as to the prevalence of pins in the tyres of machines, several competitors having to stand down owing to this cause. This trouble has been rife throughout the week and if the playful authors of the 'joke' had been found a warm time could have confidently been expected – and realised.*

Not sure, but I think that means that had they found whoever had strewn the race track with nails they would have meted out to them a punishment of the type later associated with the Hells Angels – who are always happy to hand out a 'warm time' to those getting in their way. Only they'd have done it while wearing tweed and speaking beautifully.

When something's right, it's right.

RACING IS HERE TO STAY

And boy, did it catch on. Just a few weeks after the first official race at Crystal Palace, 12,000 spectators gathered on Wednesday 19 March to watch the Charity Sports at Aston track, a banked cycle track in the grounds of Aston Hall, already home to Aston Villa Football Club. And the most popular item on the programme was the five-mile handicap for motor bicycles. Although some felt that the handicap system rather obscured the chances of a nail-biting finish, because the riders were spread out around the banked oval, there was confidence that yet more fiddling and tinkering with the rules would soon see closer racing. There were more teething problems. One being that unlike racing cyclists who wore different colours to make them instantly recognisable to the watching crowds, the motorcyclists went out with only a small, numbered card pinned at the bottom of their coats. As a result, many of those watching soon lost track of who was who and gave up altogether. Had they been following the action they would have seen that already there were stars and committed racers emerging. A certain H. Stones of Lincoln, the same H. Stones who had won at the Crystal Palace event

Miss Beatrice 'Tilly' Shilling astride her Norton at Brooklands in 1935. Not only did Miss Shilling race motorbikes, as an engineer at the Royal Aircraft Establishment at Farnborough she also invented a device that allowed Spitfires to match their Messerschmitt rivals during dogfights in the Battle of Britain.

only four weeks earlier, won the second heat at Aston on his now battle-hardened 1¾hp Rex. Unfortunately he had problems with his belt in the final – I'm assuming that's the one driving the rear wheel on the Rex and not the one holding his trousers up – and had to retire.

One thing came out of the five-mile handicap for motor bicycles at Aston that will be seen by some as ominous. I see it as a good thing: the delicious, early start of the coming divide between bikers and non-bikers. The idea was floated that competitors should be disqualified for removing the silencer from their machine. In *The Motor Cycle* this is justified because 'the noise created by half a dozen machines cycling around an enclosed track without silencers being fitted would quickly kill such kind of racing'. Nah, forget about it. Let 'em listen, let 'em hear you roar and quake in the hurricane of your coming. I would give anything, anything at all to be able to listen in to that event, to hear those tiny, fledgling engines squawking their defiance at the sky and dream of what they would turn into in just a few, brisk decades.

BROOKLANDS

Rules. We love rules. Invent a game, a sport, a machine and more time will be spent devising rules to govern it or the use of it than will be spent developing the thing itself. And the whole automobile business offered a unique opportunity for those with a predilection for carving rules from what should be the stuff of fun. Speed limits had been mooted by the joyless pretty much from the moment the first autocar had rattled out of its birthing shed. The Locomotives on Highways Act of 1896 had at least seen the speed limit of 4mph in rural areas and 2mph in towns rise to a heady 14mph. As the century had turned, though, machines on two and four wheels became capable of hitting higher speeds and their owners and, perhaps more significantly, those selling them began clamouring for the limits to be raised or even abolished altogether. Not surprisingly, they weren't abolished entirely, but in the Motor Car Act of 1903, a new limit of 20mph was imposed. It's not good then, but it is at least marginally faster, if no more reliable, than walking.

The Act also declared that henceforth all vehicles had

to be registered and display a registration number and all drivers had to have a driving licence – although there was still no actual driving test; you just bought one at the post office for five shillings. It introduced the crime of reckless driving, too, although riding a motorcycle in any manner by 1903 could only be described as a reckless act.

The question of speed and speed limits was a hot one for a long time. By 1905, unable to ignore the rising clamour from drivers and engineers alike, a Royal Commission on motor-cars was established and it reported in 1907. Interestingly it raised concerns that speed traps were being used to generate revenue in rural areas rather than as a means to secure against accidents in towns. Speed traps as revenue-raisers ... who knew?

There was, however, a silver lining to the great looming cloud of speed limits, speed traps, regulations and fines. And it was testimony to the proud, determined spirit of the pioneer motorists and motorcyclists. Realising that the speed limits were going to damage Great Britain's fledgling car and motorcycle industry, Hugh F. Locke King set about building Brooklands, the nation's first purpose-built race track. This would be a place where cars and motorcycles could stretch their legs properly, providing all the excitement craved by adrenaline-fuelled riders and drivers along with spectacle for visitors and, significantly, an opportunity for the manufacturers to test their machinery to the limit and display what it could really do, away from the nay-sayers and complainers.

It was not small. Not by a long way. And from the outset the builders realised that the track at Brooklands had to provide opportunities for spectators to enjoy the spectacle, having first

Legendary speed record holder Claude Temple poses with his gorgeous Temple-Anzani at Brooklands. Temple used the bike to set a two-wheeled land speed record of 121.3mph in 1926.

handed over their hard-earned for the privilege. The track was a banked oval 100 feet wide and 2.76 miles long. It proved to be too tricky to lay tarmac on a banked track so it was built in uncoated concrete which was, I should imagine, dreadful even at first and was only going to get worse as it settled and buckled over time. Eventually, Brooklands would grow even further until, in its heyday, it could host up to 287,000 spectators. This was it then, the Mecca at which lovers of all manner of motorised machines could join together in celebration and adoration of hot metal. It was opened in June 1907 with a posh lunch for motor manufacturers and a parade of cars around the newly-minted track. And then there were lots of car races as the whole 'society' scene surrounding the automobile intensified and grew in popularity. People gathered around car racing, just as they do today, eager to display their fashionable clothes, large watches and significantly younger spouses to a tent full of similarly equipped toffs. Motorcycling, by contrast, was a rather more down to earth affair and when motorcycle races started appearing on the calendar at Brooklands in 1908, the first races were sparsely attended. And there were more boiler suits than feather boas on display at the bike races, compared with the car events. Most of those visiting were directly involved in the actual racing, either as riders, mechanics or designers eager to display their latest idea to a crowd, even a small one. Not for the bikers the straw hats, Pimms and society chit-chat of the car world; this was about speed and performance. And as the speed and performance improved, so did the adoring crowds.

BOARD RACING

Having been there right at the very start of the motorcycle, America wasn't about to be left behind just when the thing got going properly. Charismatic inventors with simply vast moustaches and equally scaled depths of determination had been tinkering in their sheds and workshops, mirroring the efforts of their cousins across the pond. And similarly, America had seen the advantage of creating places where the new machines could be run free from the growing forests of regulations and restrictions on the road. The cycle tracks that had been used in Europe and America to host motorcycle races soon proved too cramped and flimsy for the increasingly powerful bikes and by 1901 American newspapers were reporting on European 'motordromes': circuits and tracks purpose-built to run the growing numbers of ever faster machines and host the ever bigger crowds eager to spend their money and gaze awestruck at the new breed of heroes. It wouldn't be long before enterprising American entrepreneurs set about creating their own versions.

On seeing the success of Brooklands, it was soon decided

Stateside that a race track was the place to push the motorcycle's achievements, fame and technical development while earning a handy pound – or dollar – along the way from growing crowds of eager spectators. Unfortunately, it was also decided that the cost of laying a tarmac or concrete track was too high to bear and so board track racing was invented. The banked, circular track was made of planks of wood, nailed together to form a huge, wooden bowl with spectators sitting at the top to look down on their heroes at work. By 1910 there were crowds of 10,000 or so spectators turning up at regular race meets where the riders competed for huge cash prizes. It was an amazing spectacle. The wooden bowls around which the riders raced were sometimes enormous. One such, the Los Angeles Motordrome, was built in 1910 and was described in the *Albuquerque Journal* as:

> *a perfect circle, a mile in circumference, banked one foot in three. The grand stands are placed above the forty-five feet of the inclined track. The surface consists of two by four planks laid to make a four-inch floor and laminated to give great strength. About 3,000,000 feet of lumber and sixteen tons of nails were used in the construction of the 'pie-pan' – as it has been dubbed.*

This wasn't the sort of racing we might expect to see today, then. You might well complain that charging round a perfect circle gives little opportunity for choosing a racing line, perfecting late-braking or rear-wheel steering into a tight chicane. But this was an era when simply hanging on to your 100mph bed frame with a small bomb in the middle of it was achievement enough and the sight and sound of a group of these mechanised warriors thrashing it out in an eternal circle, chasing victory down with grim faces and clenched fists while controlling their roaring steeds, rang through the public's imagination.

Excellent. So it was a huge spectacle and possessed the kind of immense-scale statistics bound to appeal to the American imagination. What the *Albuquerque Journal* didn't mention in its article about the newly-opened 'pie-pan' in Los Angeles was that the sport of board track racing, while spectacular, was also quite staggeringly dangerous for riders and spectators alike,

Americans saw Brooklands and fancied having their own track. Concrete or tarmac was expensive so they made their banked track out of 4x2in planks. Great, apart from incredibly painful splinters could be picked up in painful places if you fell off.

for a number of reasons. For starters, the bikes, by 1910, were seriously fast, often hitting 100mph. But they had no brakes. Also, they all ran 'total-loss' oil systems; essentially, the rider pumps oil to lubricate the engine and the oil then sprays off the bike and on to the track. Which was made of wood. And wood, when soaked in oil is very slippery indeed. Which meant accidents. A lot of them.

In 1912 and 1913 respectively, two huge accidents in which riders crashed off the track and into the crowd resulted in multiple deaths and injuries among riders and spectators alike. Which kind of puts a dampener on any sport. Especially when headlines like 'Thrills and Funerals' started appearing in the newspapers. As well as being grip-free to a deadly extent, the board tracks themselves started deteriorating and, not surprisingly, oil-soaked wood's combustible properties exacerbated many an accident involving hot machines and spraying fuel. In just a few short years, board track racing began, rose to be the most spectacular and exciting racing ever seen and then ended almost as quickly as it had begun.

TT STARTED

Once early motorcyclists came to realise that they would be better off if they had a place to race their bikes without the law sticking its beak in and getting all cross when they achieved their dreamed-of 'mile-a-minute' target on the road, it was only a matter of time before race tracks sprang up across Great Britain, Europe and America. Some of these, like America's board tracks mentioned earlier, were disastrous and came quickly to an end on account of them seeming to kill pretty much everyone involved with them. Others went on to great success, attracting huge crowds eager to watch the emerging legends of the day. Call them circuits, tracks or motordromes, they all had one thing in common: they were a place for bikers to congregate. Riders, mechanics, enthusiasts and dreamers could gather and share their growing passion. But the pioneer bikers, having realised the unicorn of their dreams in the motorcycle itself, were not going to stop at that and by 1907 they were to find themselves with somewhere even bigger and better to indulge their speed-crazed, petrol-charged adrenaline rush: an entire island. Back then the Isle

Jimmie Guthrie takes the flag for the 1934 Senior TT, adding another win to his tally of six on the Isle of Man. Killed racing in Germany in 1937, Guthrie is immortalised by the 'Guthrie Memorial' on the TT course.

of Man was just a rain-soaked patch jammed in the drizzle between England and Ireland. Today it is the site of the oldest motorcycle racing circuit in the world and is conceivably the place that is most closely associated with bike racing. And perhaps most surprising are the origins of the now legendary Isle of Man Tourist Trophy.

Toffs didn't generally ride early bikes. They drove cars. And the early automobiles quickly attracted around them a veneer of society style and money. Early car races were an opportunity for the working chap to stand in awe and watch the toffs trying to kill themselves in their terrifyingly expensive new

They don't name them like this any more. Sir Robert Arbuthnot, RN poses next to his machine after a third place in the 1908 TT. Sadly Sir Robert and his bike were lost at the Battle of Jutland. Fancy taking your racing motorcycle to war with you. He must have loved that bike.

machines. Each weekend, many fine old families risked coming to an abrupt halt on account of Charles Fotherington Smythe having binned his Napier into a banking. But bikers, well they were doubtless seen by the glitzy glamour-pusses of the car world as an altogether rum lot. Which makes it all the more surprising that the TT was, itself, born with something of a silver spoon in its mouth.

In 1904, car enthusiasts were suffering every bit as much as pioneer bikers under the stringent speed limits and newly forged regulations affecting their pastime. Even the recently raised limit of 20mph was holding back development of the machines and, perhaps more importantly, spoiling all the fun. Everyone who could afford a car or a motorcycle wanted to see if theirs was faster than the next chap's. And everyone who couldn't afford a car or a motorcycle was quite interested to watch those who could kill themselves in trying to find out. The Gordon Bennett Cup was a high-level, very glamorous car race that was going to be held in Germany that year and the Automobile Club of Great Britain and Ireland was keen to select a team of drivers to enter the gruelling 350-mile challenge. It was, of course, quite a posh event, given that the cars each cost unimaginable sums and the whole thing had a glamorous, pan-European feel to it. But in order to find out which drivers and which cars were best positioned to uphold the nation's honour in this international event, they had to hold trials. But where could they do it? They were banned by law from sorting it out on Britain's roads so the club secretary, Julian Orde, nipped over to the Isle of Man to visit his cousin, Lord Raglan. Of course he did. Had this been the motor-cycling fraternity trying to sort a team for an international race they might, at best, have been able to go and see a bloke called Nigel about riding around his fields. So Orde trickled over to the Isle of Man, borrowed his posh cousin's posh Daimler and wafted about the island looking for somewhere he might hold an event to sort out which were the fastest and most reliable cars and drivers they could enter. The fact that Manx laws meant racing on the roads he eventually chose was illegal seems not to have deterred him. It was a mere detail and his cousin, Lord Raglan, sorted it out for him by having a word in the right ears. Of course he did. Pesky laws. The route he had chosen took in some fifty miles of the roads linking Douglas, Castletown and Ramsey and included a tricky mountain section around the slopes of Snaefell that would really sort the chaps from the oiks when it came down to it.

In fact, only 11 cars started the event he organised in May 1904, but a lot of people came to watch so it was considered a success. Meanwhile, having watched their well-heeled four-wheeled counterparts take over an entire island to prepare for their international race, the motorcyclists were ready when their opportunity came to compete in their own international event in 1905. They nipped over to the Isle of Man and joined the cars in May to sort out who they would enter in that year's International Cup race in France. The 52 miles chosen for the cars was considered a bit of an ask for the bikes and they reduced it to 25, although it still took its toll. The whole event, in fact, proved to be exactly the sort of tough testing environment both car drivers and bike riders were after.

Of the 11 slated to start, only seven actually left the line for the five laps of the course that would decide who would have the honour of representing their country in France. The roads were due to be reopened to the public at 8 a.m. and by that time only two motorcycles had actually finished their laps. And of the three chosen to race in France, absolutely none finished the event. The following year, the car boys were too late returning to the Isle of Man for the bikers to piggyback on their visit for their own testing and they certainly weren't able to afford to arrange it themselves, so they borrowed the fields around a big house in Lancashire and did the best they could. Which wasn't enough and they were trounced once again in

the 1906 International. An ignominious start then, for bikes on the Isle of Man.

But then there was another twist and, thankfully, another toff to step forward and help them out – and a French toff, no less. There had been grumblings of displeasure from the British motorcyclists about how riders on the Continent were fitting increasingly large engines to spindly frames to comply with the overall weight limit of 50kg. Not sure what they would have made of the 1992 Honda Fireblade then. Quite a few Brits felt that this was the wrong way for biking to go and one of them, Walter Staner, the editor of *Autocar* and a keen

Team photo of the British squad in the 1906 International Cup Race with Charlie Franklin and brothers Harry and Charlie Collier.

motorcyclist himself, suggested to the Auto Cycle Club that they had an international race of their own to promote touring motorcycles rather than these frighteningly lightweight racers being pushed on the Continent. A few other chaps toyed with the idea on a train journey back from the less than successful British campaign in the 1906 International Cup. They were Henry Collier, who had founded the Matchless company, Freddie Straight, who was the secretary of the Auto Cycle Club and the Marquis de Mouzilly St Mars, a French aristocrat fluent in several languages and himself a keen motorcyclist. When I said toffs didn't generally ride bikes, there were exceptions to this rule and thank goodness for that because the marquis lent his considerable sway to the cause and founded a Tourist Trophy on the Isle of Man for 'a race for the development of the ideal touring motorcycle'. He even provided the actual trophy itself, the figure of Mercury standing on a winged wheel.

The course was just over 15.5 miles in length and the riders were to cover 10 laps. And it was pretty tough going. The road surface was far from today's velvety asphalt and they had to cope with ruts and slippery rolled tarmacadam between hedges and trees. Early riders were hitting 60mph though, tearing down twisting country lanes, wrestling with recalcitrant machines that often failed – which was exactly what the trials were about in the first place. Running repairs would include the inevitable punctures and riders carried kits with them to be ready. In fact, the riders had to be their own mechanics in a number of ways: the valve stems when hot would expand, which could effectively reduce or even cancel out valve clearance so they carried a file to file down the end of the stem once it had heated up. Not sure how happy modern racers would be about that today. Neither would they be ecstatic about the leather final drive belts that regularly snapped and always stretched until, after a lap or so, the rider would have to dismount – assuming he wasn't already off the bike trying to push it up the hill because the single gear proved too tall for the climb – and remove a section of the belt to tighten it. And they certainly wouldn't be overjoyed with the setup for the practice sessions in the two weeks leading up to the first race. It wasn't felt necessary to close the roads for practice and, interestingly, parts of the car and bike circuits overlapped, which meant that during practice sessions it wasn't unheard of for a motorcycle rider to encounter a car on the same road, COMING THE OTHER WAY. If that doesn't ask questions of your stiff upper lip, I can't imagine what does.

Aware that some aspects of the course were, perhaps, a little too testing, the organisers tried to ease matters where they felt they could. Not always successfully. The dust lying on what were just country lanes, after all, was an issue and to try and keep it down they sprayed the roads with an acid solution. It didn't work. What it did do was burn holes in the riders' clothes and boots. An interesting diversion, I'm sure, when travelling at 60mph between trees and hedges on a machine that sometimes seemed wilfully keen to kill you anyway.

The First TT, Tuesday 28 May 1907

This then, was it: zero hour, genesis, the birth of a legend that is with us still today. And there was, unsurprisingly, some bickering about the rules. The organisers enforced no weight restrictions but they weighed the bikes anyway – probably because they had some scales big enough to do the job and it would give them something to write down in a big book and look at later. There had been a rule in place governing the size of the fuel tank. But as none of the bikes seemed to have a tank big enough to meet the rule, they changed it and agreed that all riders would attend an obligatory fuel stop halfway through the race where they could refuel with the remainder of their allotted allowance for the race. This meant a lot of time in practice was spent experimenting with gearing and

Charlie Collier, on a Matchless machine as usual. He won his second TT in 1910.

carburettor setup for maximum efficiency as well as optimum speed. And the great day came, race day number one.

It was unusually cold; no doubt the riders were glad of their tweed jackets and trousers. The business of setting off alongside their machines at a run before letting go of the valve-lifter and jump-starting their clutchless bikes from cold will have warmed them up a bit too. The field was started at intervals – something that has become a TT tradition – with riders setting off in pairs. Twenty-five of them set off. There were crashes, there were fires, there was confusion about who was leading, there were snapped belts, punctures and failures, but of the 25 that started, 11 made it to the finish and Charlie Collier, son of Harry Collier, the founder of Matchless and one of the three chaps on the train back from Austria who planned the event, won the single-cylinder class on his Matchless and the honour of being the first name inscribed on the Tourist Trophy. Rem Fowler won the class for twin- and multi-cylindered bikes, despite falling off twice in the race, but there wasn't a trophy for the multi class and so glory slipped his grasp until he was in his mid-seventies when, at a dinner to celebrate the 50th anniversary of the TT in 1957, he was finally presented with a specially commissioned award.

Despite the punctures, cars coming the other way, stretchy valve stems, tweed riding kit, push starts and confusion, the event was hailed as an immediate success. Now that is how to start a legend.

Option 2: Fight with it

It's another strange but immutable fact concerning chaps that they will, having raced whatever things you have left them alone with, next turn to devising ways of fighting with them. Fencing with improvised newspaper swords, throwing Frisbees at one another's heads, it's all an extension of the same primal urge driving them to compete head to head on a race track – or down the stairs on an ironing board – only it can all get a bit out of hand. The motorcycle was, inevitably, pressed into military service when still blinking in the light as a newborn.

Racing, then, was already going well by 1902. Vast crowds were turning up at events, clutching programmes bearing the suddenly familiar names of a new breed of heroic motorcycle racers. The first motorcycle yobbos were rampaging around those races scattering nails on the track and making a nuisance of themselves while others were doing great work by complaining about the noise made by these early racers and giving the first generation of bikers something to rebel against. The motorcycle's military career, by contrast, got off to a much gentler start. Horses were, of course, the preferred and

Makes your optional heated grips look a bit dull. How about an anti-aircraft gun? These Russian soldiers are looking for enemy aircraft to shoot down early in the First World War.

A spot of machine gun practice for these Canadian soldiers in 1917. The bike seems to have a unit number on its tank but it's likely to be an Indian machine.

only means of transporting guns, troops and messages about the battlefield by 1902. But the first inkling that a machine propelled by an engine might well be a handy thing when it became time to kick the bejeezus out of your neighbours or teach a lesson to some uppity foreigners in some far-flung field was just taking form in the minds of engineers across the world. It was mooted gently at first, as it would have been a startling and perhaps embarrassingly radical suggestion to float before the ranks of moustachioed marshals accustomed to sending their troops off in mounted splendour, mirroring the glories of old from King Arthur to Waterloo – and who would consequently be perhaps less than open to the idea of sitting

Russian soldiers prepare to attack on the southern front in Ukraine in July 1942. Russian bikes look just the same today. I know, I've got one. It's terrible: I wouldn't want to go to the shops on it, let alone into battle.

their men astride what appeared to be some sort of printing press and sending them puttering off to war wreathed in blue smoke and the futile hope that they'd be at the battle before the opposition chalked it up as a no show and packed up and went home.

But the signs were that the military was perhaps starting to see the value in the new breed of motorised machinery. As *Motor Cycling* reported on 2 April 1902:

> *The Military experts of the Continent have for several years looked upon the mechanically-propelled road vehicle as a most desirable adjunct – if not an actual necessity – in*

their vast offensive and defensive schemes and the officials
of the British War Office have also turned their attention to
the same question.

The duty of proving the worth of the motorcycle as a military machine seems to have fallen first to one H.W. Duret. And he owed his big chance to a Captain Pretty of the Suffolk Volunteers. The gallant captain had elected to use a motor-cycle 'for the purposes of carrying despatches and scouting' during Easter manoeuvres. Three columns of military cyclists were charged with moving from Norfolk, Suffolk and Essex and advancing during Good Friday and Saturday on London. Perhaps the prospect of his fellow warriors advancing under pedal power had already softened any residual resentment he may have felt at the idea of relying for communications between the ranks on a civilian with a moustache and what the commander of the force engaged in the operation, Major Cadell, called a 'steam bicycle'. To be clear, it wasn't a steam bicycle that was to propel H.W. Duret between the advancing forces. He was mounted on a Singer. And while doubtless keen as mustard to prove the value of his preferred pastime to the military, he does seem – judging from his account, reported in *Motor Cycling* – to have spent the duration of the exercise riding around composing poetry.

'Despatch, despatch!' was ricocheted along the crowd.
They had guessed the truth. There was a thud on the
ground as the plump policeman stepped aside and smiled
condescending acquiescence at my departure.
'Teuf-Teuf,' said the spirit of petroleum.

'Good day, sir,' said he with the despatch.

'Good day,' said the commander of khaki, and I was
well on the road to Newmarket.

He seems to have slipped into a fairytale. But he put his
back into the work, nonetheless. In total, he covered 305 miles
over the four days of the exercise 'without any mishap or
trouble with my motor'. And he wasn't afraid to give it the
beans in fine style, the better to show off to the gazing ranks
how his powerful machine might represent an essential tool to
them in times of war – albeit a machine in this instance being
ridden by a man with his mind more on metre and metaphor
than manoeuvres:

'Teuf, Teuf,' I am near them, and they extend for half a
mile, led by Captain Pretty on a tandem bicycle. 'By your
left,' roared an officer. Putting the despatch between my
teeth, so that all might visibly appreciate the urgency of
my errand, I dashed past the column at full speed, while
they cheered me lustily.

Indeed, the troops seem to have caught on with
satisfying alacrity to the benefits of the motor bicycle
– benefits perhaps made the more urgent and apparent
to them by the contrast with their own pedal-powered
bicycles.

...I made for London, passing many hundreds of
cyclists forming the defending force on my way, many of
whom beseeched me to 'throw out a tow-rope'.

But the Great War was still twelve years away, plenty of

time for H.W. Duret to persuade the military that the motorcycle was the way forward and to work on his prose.

Meanwhile, the race was still very much on.

T.E. LAWRENCE

It's rare to see a motorcycle pictured in the popular media without a celebrity sitting on it. Generally speaking, the celebrity in question is gurning at the camera from under a well-groomed hairstyle, trying hard to exude an air of relaxed nonchalance mingled with a bit of danger, while in reality they are sitting on a bike because the agency suggested it and they secretly hope to rub a bit of the too-shiny glitter off their star with the manly abrasiveness of leather and speed. The celebrity seen perched on the latest Triumph, BMW or whatever possibly doesn't know a twist grip from a hair grip, but they're on a bike and cool people in movies ride bikes, the cool kids in the sixth form turned up to school on bikes, so bikes are cool and they too, by association with bikes, must be cool.

Beckham is pictured in the popular press commissioning a multi-gazillion-pound custom-built creation every week, Ewan McGregor is in constant danger of bumping into himself on television coming the other way on the long way down, round, up and/or over the world on a BMW and Tom Cruise could shoehorn a shot of himself grimacing over the bars of

Soldier, archaeologist and writer T.E. Lawrence, better known as 'Lawrence of Arabia', was a huge motorcycle fan and particularly liked Brough Superior machines, owning eight of them.

a superbike into a school nativity play. Net result: people who like watching football and looking at well-groomed men in their underpants believe that bikes are cool; every accountant commuting across the wilds of Kensington does so on a Dakar ready BMW GS and an action movie isn't an action movie without a bike in it. Cool. Bikes, bikers and bike-makers like it when their hobby, passion or profession is popularised; celebrities, movie stars and footballers in expensive underpants get to be seen as ready to step outside the staid world of shiny-floored TV studios and shiny-toothed interviewers, so they're happy, and bike-makers get to show off their wares to the world. Everybody wins. Not surprisingly, the mutual benefits of a bit of celebrity endorsement have long been recognised by the biking fraternity. But like every story, it has a beginning. And it begins with a most remarkable celebrity.

The granddaddy of all celebrity bikers was one T.E. Lawrence: Lawrence of Arabia. He was the first poster boy for biking, the first famous face to be seen peeking out from under a crash helmet. Although to be fair, Lawrence's face was seldom actually framed by a helmet, on account of them not yet having come into popular usage in the early 1900s. Ironically enough, it was our hero's eventual death on his beloved Brough Superior that inspired a leading neurologist to investigate the realities of head injuries in biking accidents and the effectiveness of helmets in preventing damage to the noggin. But Lawrence's influence on us all to wear helmets is just one twinkle in a vast constellation of stars scattered across the great man's lifetime of achievements and we'll come to it later.

Lawrence was born – whisper it – OUT OF WEDLOCK – sorry, I shouted it – in 1888 in Wales. In fact, his fear of being revealed as illegitimate would stalk him all of his adult life. As a boy he was shy, sensitive and considered to be 'too delicate' to play games. He was also, and I'm not saying this is important or significant in any way, really quite short. And yet this short (he was short you know, Lawrence, possibly only 5' 5", which is three inches shorter than, er, oh yes, me) sensitive, shy boy went on to earn the respect of soldiers, warriors, scholars and, most importantly, motorcyclists across the world.

After a year or two drifting about France as a moonstruck boy, admiring architecture and thinking deep, sensitive, poetic thoughts, he studied archaeology and went on to work on excavations in Syria, Mesopotamia, Palestine and Egypt. When war broke out, the knowledge and familiarity with the Middle East and its people that Lawrence had gleaned over his years living and working among them was much valued by the intelligence service in Egypt. By late 1916, still only a second lieutenant, he became confidential adviser to Emir Feisal and went on to play a pivotal role in the Arab Revolt against Turkey, seeing action himself and proving to be a fearless fighter and an inspirational leader of men.

His fame grew back home and he was boosted to celebrity status by a 1919 exhibition, 'Allenby in Palestine and Lawrence in Arabia'. It was put on by Lowell Thomas, already America's most well-known journalist and war correspondent and, from the sound of it, rather like Lawrence in being a genuine all-rounder. When the US government balked at coughing up the cash Lowell told them he would need to film and document the war, he went to a group of Chicago meat packers, who owed him a favour for having exposed a blackmailer without being too strenuous about revealing some of the potentially damaging aspects of the story.

Lowell's exhibition featured, as well as music, exotic dancing and lectures, photographs and pictures of Lawrence in his Bedouin get up and when these proved to be a smash hit Lowell took more photographs, though this time with Lawrence standing in his Arab gear in merry old England rather than staring wistfully into the middle distance in Jerusalem before a meeting with the military governor.

By 1922 Lawrence, a keen and talented writer, had published *The Seven Pillars of Wisdom*, an autobiographical account of his experiences as a soldier, but celebrity didn't always sit comfortably with the man. Having turned down a knighthood, he worked as an adviser to the Colonial Office on affairs in the Middle East and then, perhaps not surprisingly, this essentially shy and retiring chap decided to step out of the limelight and enlist in the RAF under another name, John Hume Ross, to get some peace and quiet. Sadly his ruse was found out by the papers just a few months later, but then, after a spell as a private in the Royal Tank Corps, going under the name T.E. Shaw, he re-enlisted into the RAF and settled into a life he seemed to enjoy. He worked hard, appreciated the restrictions and rhythms of service life and kept his beloved Brough Superior, 'Boanerges', in a shed on the cadet camp where he lived and worked and rode it every spare second he could find. And it was while serving in the RAF and writing as Aircraftman T.E. Shaw that he produced 'The Road', which for me remains one of the finest and most evocative pieces of writing about motorcycles and therefore one of the finest and most evocative pieces of writing about anything, ever. Yes, he was writing nearly ninety years ago about a Brough Superior racing a First World War fighter plane, but reading it now it relates just as well to the experience of a twenty-year-old today racing a Kawasaki H2 against a Eurofighter. If there is even a tiny part of you that doubts T.E. Lawrence's credibility as a true motorcyclist, if there's even the flimsiest trace of an idea that he was jumping on the biking bandwagon for effect and wasn't the real thing, with oil in his veins and bikes in his heart, read the following and change your mind immediately.

In February 1935, Lawrence received his discharge from the RAF and moved to Clouds Hill in Dorset to enjoy a quiet retirement. He had with him one of the eight Brough Superiors he owned during his life. This was to be his last one. On 13 May he crashed it, having swerved to avoid two small boys in the road. He died on 19 May at the hospital of the RAF camp where he had lived and worked so happily. His was a significant passing. He was a well-known and, judging from the reaction to his death, much-loved man. *The Motor Cycle* devoted a page to him that week, featuring a typical photograph of the man astride his Brough and telling the story of his remarkable life, finishing with the sad reflection that, 'now, tragically, the nation has lost one of its greatest'.

BAD BOYS

I didn't start riding bikes because I thought it would make everyone like me. I started riding, in fact, in a hot fever of anticipation, thrilled at the idea that I would be viewed by all and sundry as an outsider, a rebel – and quite possibly a dangerous one. Mums on the school run would look askance at my studded leathers and wince at the tinny shriek from my bike's skinny exhaust. Old people and postmen would roll their eyes as my mates and I rolled into town and leaned against our bikes in the market square. When I was knocked off at a junction, having bounced off the car's bonnet in the time-honoured fashion and lain in the road for a bit, running the usual internal systems checks on arms, legs and back, I stood up shakily and looked at the driver. Surrounding the car were various witnesses to the accident and as I looked across the sea of patterned pullovers, smart coats and office clothes I knew with a soaring joy that it would be my fault. Of course the young biker, with his long hair and smelly jeans, was in the wrong. He must have thrown himself and his motorcycle in front of the car on purpose, just to give them a scare, and he must be made to pay for the damage he had done to the innocent driver's car with his own body and his own bike. The police agreed. It was my fault. My bike lay dead in the road but I knew I would fix it up again and we would ride, together, to my mate's house and share this latest piece of proof that we, the bikers, were on the outside, where we belonged.

This was the early eighties, long after the glory days of the real biker bad boys. But there remained enough of a trace of the reputation once enjoyed by the leather-jacketed to render me and my friends on our bikes just unpopular and scary enough for our own satisfaction. The trail to this reputation, though cooling by then, was long and twisting. Despite a million heavy metal album covers suggesting otherwise, the motorcycle was not born as a red-eyed demon. There's no immediate reason why someone on a motorcycle should be viewed as a threat, as a symbol of rebellion and evil. It just sort of unfolded that way.

The pioneer motorcyclists of the early 1900s, in pursuing their passion, were not taking up satanism or crime. Of course it was possible to upset the locals on a bike. And you probably didn't have to try very hard. Just riding into town not wearing a tie could provoke disapproval. Lob in a loud exhaust and then wind the machine on a bit so the speed looks good and you're there. Presumably those early bikers were looked upon, as bikers are today, as a bit mad to choose a dangerous form of transport that involves getting wet and cold in bad weather, too hot in good weather and knocked off by cars and lorries in all weathers. If motorcycling and motorcyclists were not seen as inherently bad, they were seen by the rest of society as an odd bunch, perhaps, with their own funny interests.

Right from the start, people got together around bikes. It

started out of necessity: if you went out on your bike in the early days it would break down – always – and you would need to know what to do to get it going again. And you would need tools and expertise to do that. Pioneer bikers had to gather together to share the knowledge and experience they needed to give their next trip a hope of starting and ending in the right places. Any bunch of people gathering to engage in any activity, from a football match to a baby shower, can look threatening to those not part of it. Backs turned, all eyes engaged on something you don't understand or haven't been invited to watch, speaking a language unfamiliar to you; it all adds up to tell you that you're an outsider.

Naturally, having gathered to discuss how to stop a motorcycle's wheels collapsing at speed or the engine blowing up on hills, early bikers would enjoy some relaxed time shooting the breeze, maybe even riding out together – until a wheel collapsed or the engine blew up. And so those gatherings took on a social nature. And they grew.

Before the Second World War the American Motorcyclist Association used to run something called the Gypsy Tour motorcycle rally every 4 July, in a town called Hollister in California. They were social gatherings, with some racing and general partying. You've just read the word 'partying' in a book about motorcycles and some deep part of your brain will have overlaid images of fires and crazed drinking and chickens living in fear of their heads being bitten off. No, 'partying' means what it generally means; getting together for some fun. The rally was cancelled during the war due to the young being preoccupied in Europe and the Pacific but in 1947 the AMA decided to restart the Hollister event. It might

Previous page: The Michaux-Perreaux steam velocipede, one of three contenders thought to be the first motorcycle. Experts are still arguing about it but it is thought to have been made in 1867. It would do about 9mph but it did keep your bum warm and as it was powered by alcohol you could always have a drink if it broke down. **Above, top:** Here's another candidate for the title of first motorcycle. It's steam powered like the Michaux-Perreaux and was built by American inventor Sylvester H. Roper. The saddle served as a water tank, which was heated by a firebox burning charcoal. If it conked out you could always have a barbecue. **Above:** The Daimler Reitwagen, built by Gottlieb Daimler in 1885, is considered by many to be the first real motorcycle because it was powered by an internal combustion engine burning petrol rather than a steam engine.

Above: Pondering my 1927 Sunbeam and trying to remember how to start it and where the throttle and brakes are. It's the oldest and slowest machine in the Hammond collection, but it's loved just as much as the modern quick stuff.

Below: T. E. Lawrence's last Brough, a 1932 SS100. Lawrence – soldier, archaeologist and writer, better known as 'Lawrence of Arabia' – was killed on his SS100 while riding from his cottage in Dorset to his local post office. He swerved to avoid two boys on bicycles and lost control. He was only forty-six years old.

Above: Rockers congregate on Chelsea Bridge in 1964, possibly before a 'burn-up' to the coast or to the legendary Ace Café on London's North Circular Road. Note the lack of protective headgear, as we're still 11 years away from the compulsory helmet law in the UK.

Left: Marlon Brando poses on his bike in a still from the 1953 film *The Wild One*. The film was directly inspired by the Hollister riot six years before and played a big part in generating the bad-boy image of motorcycling in the fifties and sixties. It's not a great film.

Left: The coolest biking film ever made. Peter Fonda and Dennis Hopper star in the 1969 classic *Easy Rider*. Not only was it a great bike film, it was one of the pioneering road movies.

Below: This shot from *Easy Rider* shouts freedom and the open road. Think I'd pass on the chopped Harley-Davidsons, especially Fonda's with the ridiculously long front forks, but the image just makes you want to go out and ride.

The first-ever Yamaha, the YA-1. It was a copy of the DKW RT 125, the first German motorcycle, but the YA-1 was far better quality and had a four-speed gearbox instead of a three-speeder. In 1955, when the YA-1 was launched, nobody would have predicted Yamaha's amazing future.

Soichiro Honda, a genius and virtually the inventor of the modern motorcycle, leads his workers on one of his bikes in 1967. Mr Honda died in 1991 aged eighty-four.

Left: World Superbike rider and 2015 champion Jonathan Rea saving his Kawasaki ZX-10R's front tyre.

Above: The original 1985 Suzuki GSX-R750. Widely considered the father of the modern superbike, the GSX-R started winning races straight out of the crate. The Gixxer legend was born.

Suzuki was very late to building big four-stroke bikes but when it came up with its first, the 1976 GS750, it hit the ground running. Elegant, smooth and easy to tune for racing, the GS was an instant hit.

Mike Hailwood poses on the amazingly complicated Honda six-cylinder 250 on the Douglas promenade in the Isle of Man, sometime in the mid-1960s. Only Honda could make a bike like this and make it win.

Right: The motorcycle world fell back in amazement when in 1969 Honda launched its CB750. Four cylinders, a disc brake and electric starter.

Below: Naturally, Honda took its new CB750 racing and here's American Dick Mann on his way to winning the 1970 Daytona 200 on a tuned CB750.

have been ex-servicemen blowing off excess adrenaline from battle, or the then undiagnosed post-traumatic stress disorder, but the partygoers got a bit carried away. Just high jinks, but the press, suddenly short of exciting stuff to write about, got even more carried away than the partygoers and told tales of riots and devastation. Actually, any damage done was fairly minor. 'Some young people with a shared interest got together to have a laugh and let off some steam' does not make for a good newspaper story. Some spice was needed.

There's nothing like a good photo to back up a story and *Life* magazine's snapper set up a shot in which a fat bloke with a big belly sat on his Harley, shirt open and holding a beer bottle. Underneath his bike were dozens of empties, put there by the photographer. The image went viral, or the 1947 equivalent, and the image of the outlaw biker was born.

Say something is so often enough and it sometimes will become so. Perhaps it was on account of those early signs of a burgeoning bad-ass reputation, perhaps it was because they were cheap to run, but whatever the reason bikes found favour with less savoury types as well as those looking to save a shilling, develop their engineering skills or just experience the rush of the road. In March 1948 in San Bernardino, California, the Hells Angels Motorcycle Club was founded. The 'Angels' would go on to become as much a part of 1960s culture as The Beatles, funny-smelling cigarettes, weird music and free love. The idea of a daughter hooking up with a Hells Angel struck fear into the hearts of middle-class Americans. They'd rather have had Fidel Castro around for tea and taken him to the country club. What started as a California-based club gradually spread across the US throughout the sixties. And further:

in 1961 a branch, or chapter to use the correct H-A term, was set up in Auckland, New Zealand, with London getting its own Hells Angels in 1969. But be under no illusion that the Angels were reluctant villains. Legendary 'gonzo' journalist Hunter S. Thompson spent time with a chapter and quickly learned that their willingness to talk to him and court publicity sometimes led to their notoriety being ahead of their actions. Hell, they loved being portrayed as bad-ass in the press.

One of the most famous Hells Angels incidents was the Altamont Speedway Free Festival in December 1969. Intended as a West Coast equivalent of Woodstock, it turned out to be a very different scene to the earlier festival, where peace and love had wafted in the air. Santana opened and were followed by Crosby, Stills, Nash & Young, with the Rolling Stones as the final act. The gig was organised and thought up by San Francisco band the Grateful Dead. Not surprisingly, because it was free, lots of people turned up. About 300,000. The crowds swamped the place and there were worries that the stage, which was only a few feet off the ground, would be overrun. So someone suggested that it would be a good idea to use the local Hells Angels as security. The bikers were just meant to sit on the edge of the stage to put people off jumping up on to it. Payment for this service: $500 worth of beer.

Altamont was practically a riot, albeit a riot with a great live soundtrack. Two festivalgoers were killed in an accident with a car and another drowned in a drainage ditch. And then there was the murder of Meredith Hunter, an eighteen-year-old who tried to mount the stage (he was somewhat under the influence) but was pushed back into the crowd by a Hells Angel. Shortly afterwards, Hunter returned waving a

This charming young man is at a biker meeting in Hollister, California in 1947. It was a rowdy do, but not quite as mad as this photograph implies, as it was a set-up shot for *Life* magazine. A fake, but it frightened middle America and is one of the most famous of biking images.

revolver in the air. He was stabbed by a Hells Angel called Alan Passaro, who was later acquitted on a self-defence plea. It was a sad note to the passing of the sixties era of peace and love and it cemented, rightly or wrongly, the image of the Hells Angels.

But the action was not confined to the US. The tranquil British south coast seaside resorts of Margate and Brighton were soon to bear witness to the new biker terror. The merry clutter of kiss-me-quick hats, ice cream, candy floss and sticks of rock was disrupted on the Whitsun bank holiday of 1964. Peace was shattered by thousands of teenage Mods and Rockers rampaging on the beachfronts. The local papers said rioting, but back then not wearing a hat was considered outrageous behaviour. Mods rode Lambrettas and Vespas and wore parka coats with furry collars; Rockers rode British bikes like BSAs and used oil from their leaky engines to slick back their hair. Or that's what it looked like. You can see the culture clash between lads on squeaky two-stroke scooters wearing bird-watching outfits and hard ton-up bikers dressed in leather who rode everywhere flat out. So hard that they didn't wear helmets (they didn't have to by law then).

In Margate, 51 youths were arrested and two were taken to hospital with stab wounds. In Brighton 1000 people were running amok; there were plenty of arrests and a few prison sentences were dished out. More good PR for the motorcycle movement, or to look at it another way, if you wanted to rebel, bikes were the answer.

By the 1970s, if you rode a motorcycle you would have trouble being served in a pub. You wouldn't even get through the door, which was why biker pubs became famous. They weren't particularly brilliant pubs, you were just allowed in them if you wore a leather jacket and hadn't arrived in a Ford Cortina.

There was no logic to this unofficial ban. Raping and pillaging by bikers was rare, and, besides, many figures in the establishment rode bikes. Sir Ralph Richardson, the famous Shakespearean actor and contemporary of Sir Laurence

Olivier, rode a 750 BMW everywhere. Judges, surgeons and schoolteachers rode bikes. I knew a vicar who had a Yamaha RD400.

And then slowly it began to change. Barry Sheene arrived and became grandma's favourite. He was brave, cheeky, good-looking, fun and he didn't wear black leathers. His girlfriend was a model and he drove a Rolls-Royce. He started to change the face of motorcycling. And in 1978 he appeared on the Parkinson chat show with Sir Ralph Richardson and that, in the late seventies, put you on a level with the top stars.

By the mid-1980s the image of the outlaw biker was pretty much consigned to history. The bikes didn't spew oil everywhere, the riders wore modern gear that didn't leak and, more importantly, didn't have tassels and a skull and crossbones on the back. Successful young advertising executives bought Ducatis. Tom Cruise rode a Kawasaki GPZ900R in the 1986 film *Top Gun* and everyone's mum loved Cruise. The biker image just got cleaner and cleaner. In 2004 the very nice young actor Ewan McGregor and his pal Charley Boorman rode a couple of BMW GS adventure bikes around the world and made a film about it.

Then, the moment that closed the book on bikers being nasty and dangerous: the night before his marriage to Kate, Prince William was photographed riding his Ducati 1198S Corse. The damage done by a fat man on a Harley in a small town in California in 1947 was finally undone.

BIKE FILMS

Bikes are cool. That's a fact, not an opinion. And it was a sense of cool established only moments after mankind finally ascended the stairway to greatness and invented the things. Within days of its arrival, the newly born motorcycle was creating a culture around it, encouraging a sense of belonging, an emotionally charged call to those with the soul of a wanderer and the constitution to match. If you could heft around on the back of your bike a box of spares big enough to swallow a tug boat and were prepared to brave the worst the weather and the roads could throw at you, wearing breeches, sturdy shoes and a leather helmet that simply made it easier to find your head in the event of disaster, then you were cool. Soldiers loved them, racers risked their lives for glory on them and kids worshipped them. Better still, some people hated them and they were precisely the people that those who loved them wanted to upset, so everyone was a winner.

Films are cool, too. They can take you anywhere and they're full of cool people doing cool stuff. Even the baddies. It was only a matter of time, then, before these two icons of cool came together to create the bike movie.

Not all bike movies are or have been cool. Some have been cringeworthy tripe, bad enough to give you a stomach ache and there's more about those later. Others, though, have managed to capture an element of that precious, fleeting quality that makes biking the best thing a person can do.

Easy Rider (1969)

Nineteen sixty-nine was a spectacularly cool year. Man walked on the Moon, I was born and still the year kept on giving. Its greatest cinematic gift came in the form of *Easy Rider*, Dennis Hopper's drug-fuelled rendering of the freedom and hedonism of the sixties and the film that, if not responsible for actually inventing it, certainly played its part in establishing the entire genre of the road movie. It starred Peter Fonda alongside Hopper, who also directed it, and the main themes were drugs, sex, drugs, music, some drugs and bikes. And drugs. Hopper and Fonda both rode about the place on Harley-Davidson choppers – a chopper is a motorcycle on which the frame has been altered, or 'chopped', typically to massively increase the rake (the angle of the front forks) and in every way possible make the thing look cool and be almost entirely unrideable.

The film starts with our two young rebels selling drugs that they'd smuggled in across the Mexican border to a dealer played by Phil Spector. The money they make will finance a trip from LA to the Mardi Gras festival in New Orleans. On the way they encounter hippies living the alternative lifestyle in a commune, collect a drunken lawyer played by Jack Nicholson (who won an Academy Award for Best Supporting Actor for his part) and indulge in lots of herbally-enhanced relaxation.

As they went about the business of recording for posterity the drugs, hedonism, freedom and, yes, drugs, that defined the sixties, Hopper and Fonda proved yet another truth about bikes: they can make pretty much anyone look cool. And that is another fact, rather than an opinion. Picture the daftest individual you know or have ever seen, imagine their silly clothes, their funny walk, their inexplicable hair and now put them on a massive black motorcycle with a single, evil eye at the front, hunched low over a narrow, black wheel and at the back a fat tyre packed with swagger and attitude, embraced by slash-cut, fire-breathing pipes ... You see? Any clown can look cool on a bike. Fonda and Hopper proved that because in *Easy Rider* they ooze the kind of laid-back cool that most of us would kill for. But they do it while wearing a Stars and Stripes-painted open-face helmet and a sort of Davy Crockett bushman hat respectively; teamed, in Hopper's case, with long hair and a droopy moustache. That, my friend, is the depth, power and potency of the cool that the motorcycle can bestow upon all of us.

The soundtrack to *Easy Rider* was epic, with tracks by Steppenwolf, The Band and others. Steppenwolf's 'Born to Be Wild' was mixed with the sounds of bikes' engines in the film and is considered by some to be the first heavy metal record. Yes, it's taken on a camp, caricatured image in reference to bikes, bikers and biking, but try singing it to yourself aboard a powerful bike pointing into the inky blackness across a mountain range. It still works. It does.

Watch *Easy Rider* today and you will yearn for the open

road, freedom and the soundtrack album. What you possibly won't yearn for is a chopped Harley. They look good in the film; long, low and mean with a sinister, skinny front end and a fat, meaningful rear. But even in a film that celebrates the chopper's status as a semi-mythical steed, like a two-wheeled unicorn, you can see that they are totally unmanageable. I yearned for a chopped Harley as a kid, peering longingly at pictures of the motorcycle customiser's art in my *Big Book of Bikes* with the intensity of a lioness assessing the prey that she hopes will soon feed her cubs. I even chose the chopper version of the Evel Knievel wind-up motorcycle toy over the replica of the standard, un-chopped version on which Evel routinely set off to put himself back in hospital.

What I didn't understand, and what I can only imagine must have slipped the mind of every midnight-spanner-wielding amateur customiser ever to pour their time, money and marriage into turning a perfectly serviceable Harley, Triumph or Kawasaki into a scorching chopper, is that extending the front forks to resemble two twelve-foot scaffold poles clutching a dinner plate and dragging the rake out so the whole assembly is long enough to require warning signs and an escort doesn't just 'affect' the handling of the original bike, it removes it entirely and replaces it with all the cumbersome, spiteful reluctance of an electricity pylon being manoeuvred up a spiral staircase.

The film ends badly with both our heroes blasted by shotgun-wielding rednecks. Don't let that put you off seeing *Easy Rider*, though, because when it's going good for Fonda and Hopper, with the sun shining, the music blaring and the Harleys roaring, you will get into the groove, man, you will.

Yes, you can see that the choppers don't work. But maybe the extreme challenge, incredible discomfort and insane danger which they now present their riders is exactly the sort of impossible task that raises those riders above those lesser mortals who tool around on bikes with predictable handling and functioning brakes. Maybe, in fact, it is an unconscious reference to the early days when bikes, all bikes, whether second-hand or straight from the factory, were stubborn, unreliable, dangerous mules with a well-deserved reputation for wrestling their pilots to the ground and biting their heads off. Conquering such a beast, well, that's cool. It just is.

On Any Sunday (1971)

After the hedonistic lunacy of *Easy Rider*, it was imperative that someone produced something to show that while, yes, a certain type of fearless, spaced-out wanderer could get their kicks on a bike designed only to work in a cartoon, the business of biking was actually broader, wider and more densely featured. As bikes themselves had slowly found their way to a more measured, friendly form that you wouldn't worry quite so much about taking home to your mother, so must their portrayals in the movies.

Two years after Hopper and Fonda's adventure, another great bike movie was released, a very different one that became the greatest advertisement for motorcycling ever made. If you watch it you will thank the Lord that you ride motorcycles, and if you watch it and don't ride motorcycles you will want to. The film is called *On Any Sunday* and it was shot and directed by a bloke called Bruce Brown, who a decade earlier had made a documentary called *The Endless Summer,* which did for surfing what his later film would do for bikes.

On Any Sunday is a documentary that looks at various forms of motorcycle sport in America, from motocross to road racing to dirt-track racing. The stars were Harley-Davidson-riding flat-track god Mert Lawwill, motocross maestro Malcolm Smith and an actor called Steve McQueen. McQueen, famous in motoring circles as the star of the film *Le Mans,* was a fairly good car racer. McQueen on a bike, however, was a different matter. On two wheels he had real talent and had been a member of the US six-day trial team in 1964.

The film looks at all the forms of motorcycle sport mentioned and there's some fantastic footage of dirt-track-racing crashes and interviews with the hard bastards who competed in the sport, including one who raced with a broken foot. But the highlight and most memorable part of the film was a simple scene in which McQueen, Lawwill and Smith are messing around on a beach on Husqvarna dirt bikes. Three blokes falling off, laughing and chasing, revelling in the freedom, the visceral thrill and primal release that only a bike can provide. No five minutes of film better convey the joy of powered two wheels. Perfection.

While it shines a very different light on motorcycling to the lurid, psychedelic spotlight of *Easy Rider,* perhaps it's a masterpiece precisely because it manages to avoid pulling motorcycling entirely into the mainstream. It shows some of the depth and colour of the motorcyclists' lives, it shows their skill, determination and courage, it does some work to quash the idea that anyone on a bike is a drug-crazed loon or a blood-soaked rapist on the rampage, but it also preserves the essential 'outsider' notion of the biker; the idea that this is their thing and it's not for everyone. Even the name of the film, clear and simply stated, manages to suggest that yes, you will, *On Any Sunday*, find these people doing these things on motor-cycles in pursuit of their thrills, fellowship and purpose, but it will be you finding them, as if peering over a garden wall at the folks next door who are having far, far more fun than you.

JAPANESE BIKES

This didn't really happen, but I like to think that it did. And it could have done and maybe even did, sort of. Look, I'm going to believe that it did. Okay?

Second of October 1952. A portly man leans back on his wooden chair behind a fat wooden desk and rolls his neck, struggling to run a finger around inside his stiff collar. He lights a filterless cigarette. Of course he does. His bowler hat hangs with a confident air on its peg at the crown of a coat stand by the door to his office, from where he commands a motorcycle manufacturing company. A BRITISH motorcycle manufacturing company. This, in 1952, is a Good Thing. The depression had seen off many of the hundreds of British motorcycle manufacturers who had been around after the First World War. Others had succumbed to competition from family cars that were suddenly relatively affordable, like the Bullnose Morris and the Austin Seven. Many more had gone into making the machinery that so effectively starred in the Second World War: exporting motorcycles had become close to impossible, with the danger of another shipload of new machines being sent to the bottom of the ocean by the close attentions of a German U-boat; which hardly mattered anyway if your factory and tooling had been bombed to smithereens where they stood on British soil.

Those few companies that were left in 1952 then, must be lean, mean fighting machines staffed by focused, dedicated professionals and driven by a passion that flared deep in the hearts of the designers, dreamers and valiant industrialists who had kept alive the flame of the motorcycle through the toughest of times. Well, yes and no. But mostly no. It's maybe difficult to tell at this distance, but it looks like the show was being driven more by arrogance and complacency than by unbound creativity and razor-sharp strategic thinking.

Spread on the desk in front of our valiant industrialist on 2 October 1952 is a fresh copy of *The Motor Cycle*. And it looks like it's the magazine that is the cause of his raised industrial temperature and which has led to the collar-wrenching and fag-sparking that occupies him now.

A narrow figure appears in dark silhouette at the frosted glass of the door by the hat stand and after a deferential knock another man enters the room.

'You called, sir?' He is younger and thinner than the chap behind the desk, who looks up with bloodshot eyes past a nose clearly not a stranger to the port bottle.

'Jenkins, there's a bit in *The Motor Cycle* about the Japanese making motorbikes! What on earth does that actually mean?'

And sure enough, in the 2 October 1952 issue of *The Motor Cycle* there is a half-page news story on a handful of new Japanese models. It's a small piece, hardly a great portent of doom. A quick read reveals that two of the four machines mentioned were made by a company called Fuji, part of the engineering group that included Mitsubishi.

Mitsubishi would have been a name familiar to the readers and writers of *The Motor Cycle* and to our two puzzled motorcycle industrialists. The company built the famous Second World War Zero fighter, as well as several other wartime aircraft.

Fuji's two bikes were the S-52 Rabbit, a basic scooter that looked as though it was designed to be dropped out of an aircraft by parachute and which was powered by a 147cc side-valve engine, and the gloriously named Central Silver Pigeon scooter, a much more substantial-looking machine than the Rabbit but not a lot better looking, and it too was powered by a 147cc side-valve engine.

Of the other two mentioned in the article, one was called the Cub and was a cyclemotor. Cyclemotors had been around since the invention of the motorcycle and were essentially bicycles with a small power plant fitted to the rear wheel. It was usually a pretty feeble motor, with the bicycle's chain and pedals retained so that you could give the machine a bit of a helping hand on hills. The other bike was called the Dream and of all the new Japanese bikes it was the one that looked most like a proper bike. The Dream had a 150cc overhead valve single-cylinder engine and a seat on springs because it didn't have rear suspension. It was a bit pre-war in styling and a two-speed gearbox was hardly cutting edge even in 1952. So the Rabbit, the Central Silver Pigeon, the Cub and the Dream; not exactly the four riders of the apocalypse, as far as Jenkins and his boss were concerned, scanning the pages with arched brows leering over a condescending sneer. They could hardly see a Central Silver Pigeon or a Dream overtaking the mighty Gold Stars, Dominators and Venoms that their company and those commanded by their colleagues across Great Britain produced in large numbers every day.

The Motor Cycle reported that the Cub and the Dream were both built by a company called Houda, which according to the magazine claimed to be one of Japan's leading motorcycle manufacturers. The very obvious spelling mistake reveals, perhaps, how seriously *The Motor Cycle* took these Japanese manufacturers. Houda should, of course, read Honda. And it wasn't a one-off slip of the finger on the Remington typewriter's keyboard; Houda is repeated several times in the article and in the picture captions.

'I've no idea what it means, sir. I mean, really, the Japanese, making motorcycles. It's bally hilarious. Just imagine what a fool you'd feel riding a "Cub"!'

'I know. Or a "Silver Bally Pigeon Thingumabob". Ha!'

'Hardly. We should keep an eye out for news of the invasion of the Japanese "Dream" on the television newsreels.'

'Yes. Mind you, maybe the Japs will be making television sets next, too!!'

'Scotch?'

'Yes please, Jenkins, splash of soda. And have one yourself. Unless you want to wait until the Japanese make whisky!'

They were laughing, the lords of the British motorcycle industry, laughing like drains at this first, tentative move from the fledgling Japanese motorcycle industry. To quote that tall lady in the nice dress in that film where we are supposed to try and forget that the male lead met her because he hired a prostitute, 'Big mistake. Big. Huge'.

This is my 1000cc Vincent Black Shadow. It's gorgeous, but the only snag is that I'm too small and light to start the thing. By the time I've got that big V-twin engine into life I'm too knackered to ride the bike.

They're called café racers because Rockers in the fifties and sixties raced each other to cafés on these race bikes for the road. This is my Norton Dominator café racer. It's not very comfortable to ride so the café needs to be very local. Preferably no more than five miles away.

If you were around in the seventies you'd never have imagined that one day Triumph would come back as one of the world's most successful bike manufacturers. That's what happened when the brand was relaunched in 1991 by a Midlands builder called John Bloor.

Above: A BMW like this R90S won the 1976 American superbike championship. By BMW standards it was an exciting bike; by everyone else's it wasn't really. I've got one and it's really rather nice.

Below: The fuddy-duddy image was really thrown out of the window with BMW's first attempt at a modern superbike. The S1000RR was an instant hit on the road and track. Here WSBK rider Sylvain Barrier gives his S1000RR some gravy.

If the Italians make something it has to look sexy. And the Laverda 750 SFC (top) and the Ducati 916 (above left) certainly comply with that rule. I have an addiction to Italian bikes that's getting worse by the month. There's no cure.

Above right: This is one of the most exotic racing motorcycles of all time. It's the Moto Guzzi 500cc V8 from 1955, here demonstrated by collector and ex-racer Sammy Miller at the Goodwood Festival of Speed in 2012.

Robert Craig 'Evel' Knievel in mid-flight on his Harley XR750 at Ontario Motor Speedway. Underneath him are 19 cars and a van.

Opposite page, top: Mike Hailwood came out of retirement to race at the 1978 TT riding a Ducati. They thought he'd be slow and that the bike would conk out. They were wrong on both counts. **Opposite page, below:** British superbike star Carl Fogarty propelled Ducati's 916 into legend status by winning three world championships on it. He won a fourth on its successor, the 996.

Above left: They were the Posh and Becks of their day. Barry Sheene with his future wife Stephanie McLean.

Above right: The great Joey Dunlop, winner of a record 26 TT races. The most down-to-earth racer there's ever been. Modest, shy but incredibly quick. He won his last TT at the age of forty-eight, just weeks before he died racing in Estonia.

Above: The modern era of TT racing is faster, more dramatic, scarier to watch and more downright thrilling than it's ever been.

Above: They call them 'Aliens' because their riding skills are out of this world. Jorge Lorenzo leads Valentino Rossi and Marc Márquez at Catalonia in June 2016. The thirty-seven-year-old Rossi, nicknamed the GOAT (Greatest of All Time), won the race.

Right: Mick Doohan flying the Australian flag after notching up another of his five consecutive world championships. From 1994 to 1998 no one else got a look-in.

Top: World champion with Ducati in 2007 and Honda in 2011, Stoner retired at the end of the 2012 season, at the elderly age of twenty-seven. Here he is in his prime giving his Honda the beans out of a corner.

Above: The author on his immaculate Kawasaki Z900, hoping that a corner isn't coming up.

Japanese industry had a reputation for copying others. The Japanese industrialists didn't always play by what the British industrialists would doubtless have liked to think of as 'The Rules'. The first ever Datsun car was based on the Austin 7 but they'd forgotten to ask Austin's permission. The Japanese did, however, have a soon-to-be very relevant tendency to not only copy but, vitally, to improve, develop and turn out in very, very great numbers the things that they took as their inspiration. It sure saved a lot of time that way.

But they really didn't see it coming, the leaders of the British motorcycle industry. Many of the bowler hat-wearing old duffers who ran the bike companies after the war were the same ones running the show before it. Most weren't even interested in motorbikes and when young blokes started putting on leather jackets and white scarves and began listening to something called rock and roll the old boys panicked and hid in their gentlemen's clubs; they certainly didn't see a connection with the machines being churned out in soon-to-be diminishing numbers by their old-fashioned factories using outdated technology.

After all, there wasn't much to worry about. In the 1950s sales of British bikes were booming. The Americans loved the lightweight and sporty British bikes because all they had were ex Second World War heavy old Harleys and Indians. British bikes were winning on the world's race tracks as well, so it was all great.

The old boys sat in boardrooms in the Midlands, smoked cigars and carried on as if nothing would ever change. Oh dear. I can hear her again: 'Big mistake. Big. Huge.'

HONDA AT THE TT

In March 1954 Soichiro Honda, boss and founder of the Honda Motor Co., wrote a couple of letters. Both were concerned with his intention to enter the now legendary TT race and establish his still fledgling motorcycle company as a worldwide brand. Soichiro indulged in some proper rabble-rousing rhetoric in his letter to his staff:

> I address all employees! Let us bring together the full strength of Honda Motor Co. to win through to this glorious achievement. The future of Honda Motor Co. depends on this, and the burden rests on your shoulders. I want you to turn your surging enthusiasm to this task, endure every trial, and press through with all the minute demands of work and research, making this your own chosen path. The advances made by Honda Motor Co. are the growth you achieve as human beings, and your growth is what assures our Honda Motor Co. its future.

Although he didn't forget to address the rather more

mundane issues of, I think, tidiness in the office and making sure the banks were happy:

> The scrupulous care that is required when tightening a single screw, and the commitment that refuses to waste a single sheet of paper: these are what will open the way before you, and prepare our route for Honda Motor Co. Fortunately, our outside contractors, our agents, and our banks have given us their generous cooperation.

The other letter was for the attention of the world and, more particularly, the world's motorcycle manufacturers and buyers, and in it he declared that Honda would enter the famous and prestigious Isle of Man TT races:

> Now that we are equipped with a production system in which I have absolute confidence, the time of opportunity has arrived. I have reached the firm decision to enter the TT Races next year.
>
> Never before has a Japanese entered this race with a motorcycle made in Japan. It goes without saying that the winner of this race will be known across the globe, but the same is also true for any vehicle that completes the entire race safely. It is said, therefore, that the fame of such an achievement will assure a certain volume of exports, and that is why every major manufacturer in Germany, England, Italy, and France is concentrating on preparations with all its might.
>
> I will fabricate a 250cc (medium class) racer for this race, and as the representative of our Honda Motor Co.,

*I will send it out into the spotlight of the world. I am
confident that this vehicle can reach speeds exceeding 180
km/h.*

It's unlikely that these words, powerful as they are today
with the benefit of hindsight, sparked a lot of quaking or even
much interest across the wide world of motorcycling. Perhaps
a copy of the letter arrived at the editorial offices of *The Motor
Cycle.*

'It's those Houda people again. Now they're talking about
racing at the TT.'

The letter wouldn't have had much impact in the boardrooms of Britain's motorcycle companies either. Honda was
making small bikes and the British giants like Norton, BSA
and AJS raced big 350cc and 500cc machines. Johnny European
tended to concentrate on the smaller 125cc and 250cc classes
so let them worry about the Japanese. Not that the Europeans
would have taken much notice of Honda, either.

Mr Honda was hoping to make it to the TT races very soon
after posting his letter but that turned out to be a bit optimistic
and it wasn't until 1959 that a Honda team arrived at the haven
of motorcycle racing in the Irish Sea. The regulars didn't know
quite what to make of the Japanese team. For one thing, the
newcomers turned up on the rain-lashed shores with a doctor
and a cook. Today teams turn up with nutritionists, physiother-
apists, astrologers and all sorts of specialists but in the late
fifties turning up with someone to do the cooking was unheard
of. The Honda team had also taken the precaution of bringing
their own food with them in the ships that brought the bikes
over, but unfortunately the bikes had gone rusty on the long

1961 Lightweight TT – Mike Hailwood on a Honda 125cc

sea voyage and the rice and bean paste had turned mouldy.

The Honda team – four Japanese riders plus an American rider called Bill Hunt, who worked for Honda in the States – holed up at the Nursery Hotel in Onchan, where they were fed mutton for virtually every meal. The Japanese had only brought 125cc twins for the team; the bikes were RC141 and RC142 models, the latter a new improved version of the former with four-valve cylinder heads. As well as the racing bikes, Honda had brought over some Benly C92 production bikes for the riders to use to learn the course. According to rider Teisuke Tanaka:

I rode around the course several times to memorise it, but it was so complicated that I nearly panicked. I would stop a few times for a rest and locals would come up to me. 'Are you Japanese?' they would ask. 'Where's your motorcycle from?' When I told them that it was a Honda and made in Japan they were amazed because they didn't think we were able to make motorcycles.

They were probably baffled as to why the little Hondas didn't vibrate and weren't covered in oil, too.

Honda had a mountain to climb at the TT races. Riders unfamiliar with the circuit, funny food and bikes that were newly developed. Not surprisingly, the podium in the 125 race was occupied by European riders on European machines with an Italian MV Agusta on the top step. Honda's bikes finished 6th, 7th, 8th and 11th with Bill Hunt falling off and failing to finish. A pretty good result and if anyone was still laughing and making jokes now they were pretty naïve. Veteran racers Bill Smith and Tommy Robb could see Honda's potential and wisely visited the Nursery Hotel and introduced themselves.

In 1961 Honda won its first TT race when the legendary Mike Hailwood ripped across the line first in the 125cc and 250cc races. In the latter his 250 had a four-cylinder engine. That was a pretty trick but Honda had many more tricks up its sleeve. In 1964 it produced a 250 with six cylinders and in 1965 a 125cc racer called the RC148 which had five cylinders and revved to over 20,000rpm. In 1966 Hailwood was at the TT on a Honda 500. Now chaps, this isn't cricket. It's all very well bringing along your diddy little bikes with lots of cylinders but the big 500s, that's for the Europeans. Of course, Honda won the Senior TT and did it the next year too. You'd have had to have been very stupid not to have taken note of Honda's rapid rise to success. Stupid, or running a British motorcycle company.

SUZUKI

Gixxer. Say it out loud, now; even if the person next to you on the tube or in the airport bookshop looks at you.

There, now if you said it with a soft 'G' and shivered slightly as goose bumps tickled your arms, then you're a biker. If you pronounced it with a hard 'G' – as in 'Goat' or 'Grifter' or 'Give up' – then don't, give up that is, because you're clearly not a biker but I congratulate you for getting this far in trying to understand something strange to you and ask you to read on and learn more.

The GSX-R series of Suzuki superbikes are known, among bikers, as 'Gixxers' – soft 'G', goose bumps, etc., but you know all that now. I've got one, naturally. It's an early Gixxer 11 – a Suzuki GSX-R with an 1100cc engine and one of the last of the full-bore, 'biggest is best' Japanese superbikes made before power restrictions and punitive taxes took the wind out of such bikes' not inconsiderable sails and sales. It's not my first Gixxer, nor my second, but I think this one is a keeper. It's important.

Suzuki made their first GSX-R model in 1985. A 750, this

bike is credited with being the first modern superbike. It was an immediate race winner, winning a TT and powering on to glory in superbike racing around the world. It won that TT pretty much straight out of the crate, but the company's journey to such high-octane success had been far from simple and straightforward. And it had certainly not happened overnight.

I doubt a young Michio Suzuki dreamed back in 1909, when he founded the company that carries his name, that he would one day build a machine like the mighty Gixxer. Actually, a twenty-two-year-old Michio wouldn't have imagined that one day he would even make a motorbike. Suzuki started out making weaving machines, looms, for Japan's massive silk industry. In 1929 Michio emerged from a shed with a new type of loom that sold in huge numbers around the world. However, Mr Suzuki wasn't a man to sit back and count the yen. He figured that it would be a good idea if the company made other stuff, too, just in case the market for looms frayed at the edges.

So he set about designing a car. A few prototypes were built and then the Second World War got in the way. After the war Suzuki went back to making looms until in 1951 there was a global slump, just as he thought there might be one day. Back to Plan B. But instead of pressing on with building a car, Suzuki followed Honda's example and made a small 36cc two-stroke engine that fitted to the rear of a bicycle. This 1952 machine was called the Power Free, which was actually quite a sensible name for it.

Also like Honda, Suzuki decided to have a crack at the Isle of Man TT races and in 1960 brought along some 125cc bikes and Japanese riders. It didn't go too badly, but all the bikes finished way down the field and nobody was particularly

Suzuki's racing success started on 50cc bikes, like these tiny racers screaming around an unnamed circuit in the early 1960s. Minimal power, lots of gears and ideal for the small rider. Perfect for me, in other words.

worried by Suzuki. The next year was a bit better but not a lot. And then, in 1962, Suzuki won their first TT. But we're still a long way from the fire-breathing Gixxer: the 50cc class had been invented by then and the company won it with a diddy little 50cc racer ridden by a rider called Ernst Degner. Both bike and rider were to prove important in shaping Suzuki's future. It took a lot of individuals, circumstances and world events to create the perfect storm from which Suzuki could come roaring as a world-dominating bearer of bike names evocative enough to make a full-grown biker weep. I never have, by the way; wept, obviously, because that would be soft and I've got a Gixxer.

That rider, Ernst Degner, was an engineer working and riding for East German bike manufacturer MZ. MZ's racing manager was a man called Walter Kaaden, who is the engineer credited with being one of the pioneers of the high performance two-stroke racing engine. Having been with MZ since 1956, Degner had been able to peer over Kaaden's shoulder and pick up a few tips on how to make these motors tick.

In August 1961 the Berlin Wall was built between East and West Germany. Degner didn't fancy being cooped up in the East so he made a plan. He organised for his wife and family to escape from the East one weekend in late August of that year, while he was riding his MZ 125 in the Swedish Grand Prix. Degner was leading the world championship in the 125 class and could have bagged the title in Sweden. Unfortunately, his engine conked out early in the race. I doubt young Ernst was too bothered by that because he had rather more on his plate. He literally jumped off his dead MZ, leapt into his Wartburg car, crossed on a ferry from Sweden and eventually met up with his wife and family on the French/West German border.

Not only was Degner a pretty handy rider, but his head came preloaded with lots of juicy secrets and tricks of the trade from Walter Kaaden and MZ: not surprising then that Suzuki were rather interested in him and immediately signed him up and flew him over to their race shop in Hamamatsu, in Japan, where he spent the winter designing 50cc and 125cc racing engines. A good winter's graft because, as we now know, in 1962 Degner gave Suzuki their first world championship riding a tiddly RM62 50cc racer.

Throughout the sixties Suzuki kept racing and learning about two-strokes, not all of them tiddlers. By 1971 they were making the GT750, a three-cylindered water-cooled two-stroke that looked like it had an engine from a racing bike but in fact was more of a smooth-running touring bike. It kicked out a lot of smoke, used a lot of petrol and made a fantastic noise. It became known as the Kettle in UK biker circles, something to do with its hot-running water-cooled engine, and the Water Buffalo in the States because, well, because it was quite a big bike and it involved water.

In all, Suzuki enjoyed four decades of developing and honing the two-stroke, not bothering with a four-stroke bike until they launched the GS750 in 1976. Well they did have one earlier foray into realms outside of the two-stroke universe with the 1974 RE5, which was powered by a rotary or Wankel engine. It was very complicated and must have cost Suzuki more to develop than it ever got back in sales. The 1976 GS750 evolved and got better. Other four strokes came and went and then, in 1985, the first Gixxer arrived and bikers got a new word to clutch to their leather-clad chests and croon over.

Amazingly, Michio Suzuki was around to see both the GT750 and the new GS750. Mr Suzuki died in 1982 at the grand age of 95 and I hope very, very much that he was pleased with his life's work. I know I am.

YAMAHA

One word: Fizzie. That'll have anyone who was a teenager in the 1970s or early 1980s sitting up to attention. For those who didn't grow up in the 1970s or early 1980s, it's probably difficult to see how a faintly cutesy word like 'Fizzie' can be as laden with potency, power, symbolism and significance as it is for those of us who grew up lusting after, buying, crashing, rebuilding, crashing again and rebuilding again the little moped so nicknamed. Yamaha called it the FS1-E, we called it – all of us – the 'Fizzie', but both sides would agree that it was one of the most important motorcycles ever built. It gave a generation the chance to take their first steps into the actual world of real biking rather than dreaming about it in the back of the family car. One day you had a piece of cardboard taped to the chainstay of your bicycle to make it sound like a motorcycle, the next you had the real thing. It was freedom, power, adulthood and the most sublime, seductive thing life could offer a sixteen-year-old kid. It also turned those same kids into outright liars, but more of that in a moment.

The Fizzie was technically a moped, but not like the kind of thing used by French people to collect their baguettes from the *boulangerie* in the morning. Yamaha had the vision and sense to make their 50cc wonder look like a proper bike and, most importantly, did something clever with the legally required pedals. By shifting a lever you could swing the pedals independently of each other so that they could move forward together and act as footrests. Locked into position, they weren't pedals on a moped at all; they were the footrests on your motorcycle – and they stayed there, locked. If anyone asked, you could explain that yes, they could be separated to form pedals, should the need arise for them. What you might not share is just how difficult it actually is to pedal an FS1-E and how rather than be seen on the high street grunting and straining at the pedals of your broken-down moped you would fake a heroic motorcycle accident by laying your bike on the road and chucking yourself into a hedge to wait for help to come.

In theory a Fizzie could do about 50mph but everybody used to fib about how fast theirs could go. Every village in North Yorkshire, where I grew up, had a lad in it who claimed his Fizzie had once done 70mph on the flat and touched 75mph going downhill. Let's be clear, it hadn't. But we believed him – we wanted to. If that skinny farmer's lad from Monkton could break the speed limit, break an actual grown-up speed limit on his bike, then so could we if we could just work out the devious tweaks he had made to its innermost workings. Wild claims were made and the technically over-confident would take their bike's engine to bits and try and tune it. In truth, a Fizzie has only about as many moving parts as a ballpoint pen and is easier to dismantle. And then you could lift out its internal organs to examine, to turn over in your teenage hands the very things that combined to bring about the mysterious miracle of motion.

Borrowing a spanner from your dad's garage and taking the top off your Fizzie's engine was like being allowed to open up the chest of a heart patient and have a go at fixing it. It was a sort of amateur surgery and deeply liberating. Usually the bike would go more slowly or blow up on the first run to the fish and chip shop. And then beckoned another long afternoon of sitting on the concrete next to your best mate in a pool of spanners and tea, turning over a con rod, gleaming in its visceral juices, and marvelling silently that the world

Without doubt the Yamaha FS1-E was the most important bike of the 1970s. It was technically a moped but looked like a proper bike. It launched a generation of bikers.

had accepted you, a spotty young teenager, into this realm of motion, independence and responsibility. I've got a Fizzie today, bought in a mad burst of retro-fever. It still looks cool and it still sings to my heart of teenage rebellion, of feeling my way into the world and revelling in the joyous, high-pitched scream to the skies from the bucking little beast beneath me. It won't do 50mph though. And I don't ride it much in case I get a case of retro acne.

Yamaha was started in 1887 by a gentleman called Torakusu Yamaha. Mr Yamaha didn't join the pioneers of motorcycling but chose instead – for reasons of his own – to make pianos and reed organs. It wasn't until 1954 that the company, wondering what to do with the machines and knowledge that they had left over from the war, came to their senses and decided to have a go at making something worthwhile: motorbikes. They made a machine called the YA-1, which was a knock-off of the German DKW RT125. Nothing wrong with that: stealing designs can better be described as 'taking inspiration from'. BSA 'took inspiration from' the RT125 for its Bantam – in other words they stole the design – and Harley-Davidson turned the DKW into a bike it called the Hummer. It's how things get done, so let's not get all precious about it.

Yamaha didn't swing immediately into heavy-duty, inten-sive production along the modern Japanese model. In fact they only made 125 YA-1s in the first year, but they liked the idea of making bikes, so in 1955 they formed the Yamaha Motor Company. Not wanting to forget their roots in the world of classical music, they incorporated three tuning forks into their logo. They're still used today and you can amaze your biking friends with that piece of historical knowledge. They shall register their respect and admiration for you by ignoring you and talking to someone else.

So, Yamaha had built a motorbike. There was by now a well-established pattern of what to do next: go racing. On 9 July a trio of YA-1s were entered into a race near Mount Fuji. It went rather well, with three Yammies leading until one conked out, to leave it a Yamaha 1–2. Yamaha were thrilled to bits with their success and continued racing bikes in Japan throughout the rest of the decade. They had so many successes that the name Yamaha became known not just for making very nice pianos – well, they look nice, and they are pianos – but for winning motorcycle races.

Then just as the fifties turned into the sixties something went a bit wrong. Honda hadn't had as much success racing versions of their road bikes, so around 1959 they decided to change to another plan and build bespoke machines designed for one reason only: to win races. What they did was get really serious about it. Over the next few years Honda came out with all sorts of wonderful and exotic bikes that tore up the world's race circuits, so Yamaha were forced to go back to the drawing board and come up with their own thoroughbred racing bikes. Whereas Honda built four-stroke racing bikes, Yamaha concentrated on two-stroke racing bikes (Yamaha didn't build a four-stroke road bike until the 1970s).

We'll come to the difference between four- and two-stroke motorcycle engines a bit later – it's a big subject, like most religious divisions, and worthy of proper examination – but what you need to know now is that highly tuned two-stroke engines, especially early ones, had a habit of 'nipping up'. That sounds rather nice, 'nipping up'. A person can 'nip up' the road for a paper; we speak of 'nipping something in the bud'; 'nipping out' for a swift pint. 'Nipping' in general can be a pleasant sort of thing to talk about and experience. This wasn't. Basically the piston, whose frantic leaping up and down at the speed of sound inside the cylinder lies at the heart of the miraculous process of making motion, suddenly stops dead or seizes. That's more than an inconvenience because quite apart from the imminent prospect of standing by the side of the road waiting for a taxi, the more pressing matter immediately becomes the fact that the back wheel has stopped turning with the same alacrity and determination that the piston gave up on plunging up and down its bore and chose to stop dead. There's a chance you can, at this late point, save the situation by pulling in the clutch lever and if you are a fighter pilot you might actually react correctly and quickly enough to save yourself. You won't, though – what you will do is depart your motorcycle very, very rapidly, sail through the air for a while, possibly long enough to make a comment about people looking like ants below or 'I can see my house from here' and then you will plunge head first into a hedge, a fence or any piece of unfor-giving street furniture left lying about the place expressly for the purpose of maiming riders of two-stroke motorcycles experiencing their first – and possibly last – 'nip up'. Riders of racing two-strokes always kept a finger on the clutch lever just in case this happened. Might as well keep a St Christopher medallion in the top pocket of your military tunic in the hope it stops a bullet.

Although Yamaha made purpose-built race bikes, they still kept to the plan of building racing bikes for amateur racers and non factory-supported riders that were based on their road models. Throughout the sixties and seventies the world's racetracks were full of Yamaha race bikes that weren't much different to the machines that the spectators had arrived on. The most famous of these race bikes was the TZ series. You could buy a TZ250 or 350 and an old van and go off around Europe racing your bike against top-class riders, being paid a bit of money to appear and if you were lucky take home some prize money, too. Meanwhile, on the road, bikers in the seventies were riding RD250, 350 and 400 air-cooled two-stroke twins that punched well above their weight.

And then in 1980 Yamaha dropped a bombshell and introduced a bike called the RD350LC. It had a water-cooled engine like a TZ and apart from a headlamp and a number plate it looked like a TZ. It was fast, reliable and went around corners faster than your mate's Kawasaki 900. There was a waiting list for both the 350 and the 250 version. Today the LC (that's the only letters you need to use) is a sought-after classic. It's Yamaha's most famous bike, but not the most important because it was the Fizzie that inspired the generation who went on to buy LCs to ride in the first place.

KAWASAKI

It's a sad fact that, like most Japanese bike companies, Kawa-saki didn't start out building bikes. But rather than wasting their time making pianos or harps, they were at least building something much sexier: aeroplanes. After the Second World War was over, Japanese companies were, along with German firms, asked politely but quite firmly not to make any more fighter aircraft and bombers, so things rather dried up on the aeronautical front for a bit. They dried up, in fact, until 1954, when the ban was lifted. Kawasaki have since been involved in building commercial jets, military helicopters and fighter jets, both under licence and under their own name.

Exciting as all the flying stuff was and is, the company still had the vision to go after something truly thrilling and thank-fully got into bikes in 1963, when it bought a Japanese motor-cycle company called Meguro, which had got into difficulties and was by then pretty much on its back. Kawasaki engineers helped the Meguro people finish off a bike called the K1, which was a copy of BSA's A7 500cc and was therefore probably a pretty dreadful thing. They then went on to develop a bike of their own called the W1, which was a conventional parallel twin. All pretty staid, safe stuff really. That wasn't to be the case for long. Kawasaki might have been late to the global bike party, but they weren't about to sit around being boring once they'd arrived. This was a company by now familiar with the business of building attack helicopters and guided missiles; it might be said that they knew a thing or two about building machines that could raise an eyebrow or challenge a trouser.

Just a few years later the sixties were in full swing and the Summer of Love was sizzling with spaced-out Beatles roaming the globe in search of revelation, liberation and more drugs. Maybe The Beatles dropped by Japan on their way to discover their own belly buttons in India and accidentally left a bag of Smarties behind on a whistle-stop visit to the HQ of Kawasaki. Whatever, something must have gone on that was a bit more than a dreary meeting with biscuits because in 1969 Kawasaki launched a bike called the H1 Mach III.

Mach III. Now that, marketing people, is a name. Let's not try and sketch out any pretensions to utilitarianisms here and neither let us limit our ambitions in terms of potential. Mach III. Not the speed of sound, but three times the speed of sound.

Surely the fastest name ever put on the side of a motor vehicle. The Mach III was powered by a three-cylinder, 500cc two-stroke engine that produced 60bhp. But that's just the technical description of the engine; in reality it was like having three hand grenades under the petrol tank all with loose pins.

To be a hero, you must be brave. And to be brave, you must first be scared. The Mach III then was a sort of two-wheeled detection device for identifying heroes.

The first issue was that the big 500cc engine really liked to

The terrifying H1 500 of 1969. Three cylinders of angry two-stroke power and a frame with a hinge in the middle.

be thrashed because if you just pootled about on it the spark plugs would oil and the bike would bang and fart to a standstill. So thrash it or it conks out. The second issue was that thrashing a Mach III was a very terrifying experience because Kawasaki's engineers had spent so much time developing the bike's weapon of mass destruction engine that there wasn't much time left to design a nice handling bicycle to put it in. The Kawasaki H1 was a bike that turned a dead straight road into a set of tricky corners. The frame felt like it was made out of bent milk straws and even the most talented rider struggled to control the thing. So you had to thrash it to make it work and if you thrashed it you would almost certainly end your day in a tree, hoping you were still around to hear the sirens.

The evil-handling, smoke-belching Mach III gave Kawasaki

an overnight reputation for building bikes for the clinically insane. And that was just the start of it. When Honda shocked the world by unveiling their fabulous CB750 in 1969, different manufacturers reacted in different ways. Triumph doggedly plugged on with their new, three-cylinder, old-fashioned Trident, secure in their Brummie confidence that no one would want a faster, more reliable bike with more cylinders and an electric starter. Kawasaki, on the other hand, panicked. They were also working on a four-cylinder 750, but in the face of this dazzling newcomer from Honda decided that instead of carrying on they would tear their design up and go back to the drawing board. What they came up with was another legend. Launched in 1972, the Z1 was a 900cc monster with twin overhead camshafts (the CB750 only had one), a four-stroke engine and a top speed of 130mph. Like the scary Mach III, the Z1 wasn't particularly good at going around corners but it was very fast and the engine was almost bulletproof and very easy to tune for racing. So assuming you managed to wrestle it round a corner, you could be sure that it would be pitching you up at the next fright sharpish, like a turbocharged ghost train.

While essentially crazy in most contexts, the Z1 was, by Kawasaki's standards, as sensible as bedroom slippers. Time then for another piece of sheer, unbridled lunacy. Any suggestion that the company was going straight was dispelled by a bike called the H2 Mach IV. It was essentially a 750cc version of the Mach III that was even faster and, impressively, handled just as badly. It would pull wheelies without the rider trying, making the H2 one of the first easy-to-wheelie road bikes in the world. Something, doubtless, of tremendous interest when explained to police officers; as it must frequently have been.

Being scared is a visceral, sensual thing. We can take in terror through each of our senses and Kawasaki perhaps decided that while most of those senses were being stimulated almost to the point of destruction by their machines, our sense of vision could take – and would revel in – another hefty jolt. This, they decided, would be an even more impressive feat if it could be achieved even when the bike was standing still. And the answer to that lay in a paint tin. Honda, Triumph and others painted their bikes with nice coach lines on their tanks and used gentle colours. The designers at Kawasaki went off into a dark room, put on an early Pink Floyd album, hand-rolled some cigarettes and came up with two-tone purple paint schemes, violent oranges and eventually its trademark lime green, which was first used on Kawasaki's race bikes and is used on today's road bikes.

You'll find that same lime green paint on a modern Kwacker (no biker actually calls a Kawasaki anything but a Kwacker) called the H2R. Pulling an old name out of the history books is common practice in the motorcycling world and when Kawasaki needed a name that conveyed high performance and brown trousers it couldn't do better than the name H2. The modern H2 is a mind-bendingly fast, supercharged superbike that's available in an R version which is designed for track use only. The H2R produces a ridiculous 300bhp, which is more power than the original Porsche 911 Turbo had under its bonnet.

Kawasaki motorcycles. Frightening bikers since 1969.

HONDA

'You meet the nicest people on a Honda.' That was the slogan that Grey Advertising came up with in 1963 when Honda approached the agency for help in cranking up Honda 50 sales in the US. It was a brave call. Industries generally try to focus in on the qualities that people believe their product imbues, the fantasy element that plucks at the consumer's imagination and persuades them to part with their readies. People selling razor blades show adverts featuring racing cars shooting about accompanied by rock music, aftershave manufacturers employ a man whose voice registers in an octave only audible to elephants through their feet to tell us how many panting girls we will be prising from our manly trouser legs if we splash the contents of their latest bottle on our chin. And yet here was a maker of bikes – machines whose power and appeal was, surely, wrapped up in images of leather-clad dudes sneering at old people and living a life of freedom from rules, traffic cops and soap – showing TV adverts in which immaculately dressed women cruised around Beverly Hills on a Honda 50 on their way to buy expensive shoes. Posh mums were shown taking a child to school on the back of a Honda, going to the library and all sorts of other respectable errands that in reality posh women probably did in Cadillacs. It was like Ann Summers advertising their new range of specialist underwear by photographing it on a nun. Actually ...

Never mind, because it worked. Firstly, it lifted Honda motorcycle sales to the heavens in 1960s America, but more importantly it dramatically changed the image of motorcycling. A Honda rider was polite, well dressed, used soap on a daily basis and was the total opposite to the popular image of the outlaw biker, drinking and rioting and pillaging. You didn't need to lock your daughter away from a bloke on a Honda; you might even want her to marry him.

That was all well and good but the company hadn't gone entirely soft and dewy-eyed about bikes and biking. While a growing number were pottering around on their Hondas being the nicest people, Honda were busy dominating the world's race circuits and pushing the boundaries of engine development to ridiculous extremes, with six-cylinder 250cc racers that revved to over 15,000rpm. Their eye was still on sales, though. Experience won the hard way in the ruthless crucible of motorsport was brought to bear on road bikes, too. Already Honda were building sophisticated 125cc and 250cc bikes that had electric starters so that you didn't break your ankle starting them. The engine oil stayed inside the engine rather than coating your shoes and messing up your garage floor. They didn't judder so much that your teeth became loose and half the bike was left behind on the road as bits vibrated and nuts came undone.

These shrewd tactical moves and clever, ruthlessly

pragmatic and forward-looking image-building exercises by the Japanese motorcycle industry did not go unnoticed back in the UK. The Great British motorcycle industry stirred, opened an eye, burped gently and went back to sleep. The bowler-hatted corporate moustache stands of Birmingham had probably learnt how to spell the word Honda, but they still didn't take them seriously. Honda and the other Japanese companies made small bikes that couldn't compete with 650cc BSAs, Nortons and Triumphs which you had to kick start into life, leaked oil and shook themselves to bits. And weren't even very fast. A few executives weren't quite so blinkered, including ex-Triumph engineer Edward Turner who reckoned that people would start out on small Japanese bikes, get hooked on biking then move up to big British bikes. Good theory, but Turner wouldn't have guessed what was coming.

In 1968 Honda dropped the bomb. At the Tokyo motorcycle show in October it launched a bike called the CB750. No getting round it, this was a big moment. And suddenly everyone noticed: the Japanese, who didn't make big bikes, were making a big bike. Not only that, but it was a really, really good big bike. The CB750 had a four-cylinder engine, an electric starter and a disc front brake. It was sophisticated, was obviously the product of racing technology, didn't leak oil and ran as smoothly as a watch. Back in Coventry, Triumph was about to launch a bike, too. It was a 750 also, but it had three cylinders (it was called the Trident) instead of the Honda's four, had no electric starter, used pushrods instead of a sexy overhead camshaft and had an old-fashioned drum brake. And of course it leaked oil and shook a bit. Triumph had arrived at Honda's gunfight carrying a sink plunger.

While to the eyes of the aged, flustered British bike industry Honda's large-capacity bikes must have seemed horned devils bestriding the Earth and seeking out their children for a supper snack, they were in reality still bought by nice people. The legacy of that 1963 ad campaign was alive and well and nice people bought CB750s and nice people raced them, including a bloke called Dick Mann who won the prestigious Daytona 200 on one in 1970. Racing victories, especially ones by nice people on nice motorbikes, mattered. A victory at Daytona on Sunday meant there would be a rush to dealers on Monday morning to buy the nearest road bike to the racer and the CB750 was very close to the racer. Honda sold millions of them across the globe and to some they became as familiar as milk bottles. When I was growing up in the 1970s you never heard people talk about the Honda CB750 – all they needed to say was 'my mate's got a 750 four' and you knew exactly which bike they were talking about.

Throughout the 1970s Honda kept on producing motorcycles for people who were kind to animals, including the immortal Honda 50 which went on to become the best-selling motor vehicle of all time. Actually, it's not just the numbers sold that make the Honda 50 important, it's the fact that for millions of people around the world it's what they chopped the family donkey in for. It was the first method of family transport that didn't need to be beaten with a stick to get it going. This was motorcycling as an important social tool, a means for changing the way people lived. One day, in the far, far future, someone will establish and define the specific evolutionary influence of Honda. Probably.

And then suddenly, in 1992, Honda did something a bit out

It says in the advertisement that you meet the nicest people on a Honda. And clearly you do, as these two sisters on their Honda 50 Cub in 1969 demonstrate.

of character. They built a motorbike that was angry, feisty and aggressive. It was called the CBR900RR Fireblade or 'Blade for short. Honda had pulled some amazing tricks since the 1968 launch of the CB750, like following it up in 1978 with a 1000cc six-cylinder superbike called the CBX, but the Fireblade broke new ground. It was as light as a 600cc sports bike and yet it had the power of a 1.0 litre superbike; it was extremely fast but it also went around corners well and looked fantastic. They were bought in their legions by middle-aged men desperate to re-establish and parade the virility and bravery of their youth. And they were promptly returned to the shop, sometimes a day later, when the same middle-aged road warrior realised that things had moved on quite a bit since his CB750 and that this was a different, altogether angrier, edgier beast and best reserved for the capable, steady and less heavily-mortgaged hands of the younger generation of riders in their brightly coloured race suits.

Nice people still bought Hondas, but it helped if they were brave, too. Honda had carried forward the ethos of their 1963 ad campaign without ever giving up on their ambition to make machines that were fast and exciting as well as reliable and oil tight. In the same year as the 'Blade, Honda produced the NR. This was a road-going version of their NR750 race bike that, in turn, had its roots back in 1979 and Honda's discovery on returning to Grand Prix racing that they needed to squeeze more power from their four-stroke V4 engines to keep up with the opposition's frantic, fast-spinning two-strokes. The rules limited competitors to a maximum of four combustion chambers. So Honda designed oval pistons, each driving two conrods and being served by two sets of valves. Effectively, they made their V4 a V8 without breaking the rules. It didn't work especially well – the NR was dubbed the 'Not Ready' – but they persevered and by 1992 were able to present the world with the most expensive road bike ever sold.

The most expensive until the RCV213V-S was launched in 2015, with a sticker on its windscreen that read £137,000. The RCV is as near as you can get to a MotoGP racing bike with number plates. It is one of the most sexy bikes in the world and one of the fastest. To buy one and ride it you need to be rich, talented, brave and, of course, nice. It is, after all, a Honda.

THE BRITS

A colleague of mine who must remain nameless, so let's call him James May, just as his mother did, recalled to me a meeting he had with a Professor of Birmingham from Birmingham University. Let's not get caught up now in quite why a city would feel the need to provide its own university with a professor specialising in the city in which it was based and neither let's start wondering how this strange circularity didn't engender some sort of cosmic feedback resulting in Birmingham and the surrounding areas vanishing into such a black hole as might be created by that particle accelerator affair. Let us instead ponder what the man said to my nameless colleague (it was James, James May, the one with daft hair and a habit of getting dressed in the dark in a shed). The Birmingham Professor of Birmingham said to him that 'the problem with people from Birmingham is that they like crap'. Now, this may or may not have actually been said, the meeting with the professor may never have happened and there may not even be a Professor of Birmingham at Birmingham University but the fact is, when my nameless colleague called James May told this story, true or untrue, it generated a lot of raucous laughter that carried with it more than a suggestion that the people who were present agreed with the idea; that it resonated with them and that they were willing and ready to believe that the good folk of Brum preferred crap to better stuff. Why else, they would ask, should anyone choose to live in or even be from Birmingham?

Hurtful, I know. Especially so for me because I am from Birmingham. And no, I don't like crap. I like expensive watches, beautiful cars, well-trained dogs, well-mannered people and well-fitting clothes. Problem is, I also have a penchant for old British bikes. And this is a problem for me to admit in the face of the observation from the Birmingham Professor of Birmingham because they are, by and large, crap. And the terrible truth of the matter is that whatever their preferences, the good folk of Birmingham and the surrounding area have made, alongside a lot of wonderful, timeless stuff, quite a lot of what really can only be called crap. Especially when it comes to dropping an engine between two wheels and fitting it with handlebars.

Why, when other British factories were working on magnificent things like Concorde, the English Electric Lightning fighter, Lotus Formula One cars and Marshall amplifiers, was the British motorcycle industry presenting the world with wheezing, under-powered, poorly styled, oil-spewing rattlers?

Some readers may have left us at this point. There are those whose watery eye ducts are connected directly to the notion of an old British motorcycle, just as there are those who hanker after better times gone by when chips came in newspaper, rickets was fashionable and the community spirit was heightened and tightened by the sporadic arrival of bombs from the sky or the appearance of a violent thug in an East London pub who knew proper values and broke your knees with a proper working-class passion. These people will be cross with me and I apologise for insisting that we face up to the reality of it. The fact is that after the war, the British motorcycle industry was largely in decline and with good reason. Its bikes were, by and large, well, they would have found favour with the Brummies in the story from the Birmingham Professor of Birmingham.

I have already stuck the boot into the old biffers who ran the British motorcycle industry after the war, and in truth they do deserve a bit of flak. It can't have been the engineers, toolmakers and craftsmen, it must have been the management. And anyway, the blame must always filter upwards: somebody said yes to the designs, to the corner-cutting, cost-saving and dreary styling and that somebody was, without doubt, the daft Herbert in charge.

But it wasn't all a complete disaster and we can't throw the entire British bike industry into a skip. Really, we can't. They may have been washed around the world lost in a tsunami of dreary rubbish, but some good machines did come out of Brit factories. And then there were some brilliant ones. Take Vincent, for example. The company was founded by a chap called Philip Vincent in 1928, or to be more accurate, Phil bought the collapsed HRD motorcycle company and renamed it Vincent HRD (dropping the HRD bit after the war so as not to confuse it with the H-D of Harley-Davidson). The most famous model that Vincent made was the Rapide. And the ultimate version of the Rapide was given a nickname on account of its black-painted engine casings. In a rare moment of fizzing inspiration for an industry that prided itself on pulling out of the air a name that always somehow conjured up images of rain-soaked cobbles, poor plumbing and lumpy gravy, for even the coolest and sexiest product, Vincent called its machine 'The Black Shadow'. Giving a motorcycle a name best suited to a superhero was a bold call, but it was justified. It was, and still is, bloody amazing.

It's powered by a 1000cc V-twin engine that produces about 55bhp. That's not much poke but the big motor has a lot of torque and therefore the Vinnie – I know, the ease with which I dash off its pet name suggests closeness and familiarity; it's because I've got one – had a top speed of around 125mph. And it didn't hang around getting there. The whole package added up to something more than the sum of its parts – even the brakes worked – and it managed to remain the fastest production motorcycle in the world long after the company making it went, inevitably, out of business.

You can spot a Vincent owner not only by their confident deployment of the term Vinnie, but also by their possession of an unusual right leg. This limb will be far more muscly than the left one, often twice the size, due to kick-starting the bike's engine. Some Black Shadows were treated to a Lightning specification which, among other things, meant raised compression, making the kick-start procedure something close, in terms of effort expended, to the business of transporting a space shuttle to the launch platform and then hurling it into space. Mine, the one that I have here at home in my garage, has the Lightning specification engine and because I'm short and have a perfect athlete's physique I do struggle with starting it and

The legendary Rollie Free breaking the American bike speed record at 150.313mph in 1948. His specially made leathers had torn at 147mph so Rollie binned them and rode in Speedos, bathing cap and trainers instead.

little short of leaping from the top of a high wall on to the kick-start lever will succeed in moving the thing through even a fraction of a degree. Worth it when it goes, though, because it's a wonderful thing.

What is perhaps the most famous photograph in motorcycling involves a Vincent. It's of a bloke called Roland 'Rollie' Free breaking the land speed record for bikes at the Bonneville Salt Flats in Utah in 1948 at 150.313mph. Rollie was a pretty determined bloke, as evidenced by his approach to nabbing the speed record on the Vinnie. He had made some special custom leathers for his record attempt but at just over 145mph the wind tore them to bits. The solution? Simple: Rollie discarded them and instead wore a pair of Speedo swimming shorts, a shower cap and a pair of trainers. Lying perfectly prone on the bike, Rollie took the record – at the cost of all dignity though not, as it might so very easily have been, at the cost of all his skin.

Vincent, following British motorcycle industry tradition, went up the spout and at the end of 1955 produced its last ever motorcycle. But the Bonneville Salt Flats, site of the company's heroic if under-dressed speed record achievements, were very much still there, singing their siren song to fearless adventurers and speed junkies as well as manufacturing industry management hungry for PR. Definitely falling into the former two categories was another record breaker, Johnny Allen, who in 1956 obeyed the call and took a machine called the Texas Ceegar to the salt flats to stretch its legs and carry him into the record books.

The Texas Ceegar was a streamliner, a term for bikes that had a form of body built around them to solve some of the knotty aerodynamic issues that arise when careering across the ground on a machine that is otherwise covered in protruding lumps and bumps which grab at the wind and catapult the rider through space or, worse still, hold back some of the last few precious mphs and deny the rider their place in history. The Texas Ceegar had a tubular frame and a fibreglass body that was 15ft 8in long and 22.5in wide in the middle. Just wide enough to insert the very brave Allen. The machine's designer, J.H. 'Stormy' Mangham, an airline pilot and bike-shop owner in Fort Worth, built the frame so that various different-sized engines, all made by Triumph in Coventry, England, could be fitted. This crafty move meant that they could break records in different capacity classes. The team had already set a 500cc record of 198.020mph in 1955 but came back the next year with a 650cc Triumph engine to have a crack at the overall land speed record for two wheelers. On 6 September brave Johnny wound the streamliner up to 214.40mph and broke the record. A light went on in Triumph's marketing department in Coventry as the company realised that this was a fantastic opportunity to sing the proud name of Triumph from every church steeple and tower in the world. Or at least in bike shops. They decided to launch a bike to celebrate, but what to call it? Of course, the Triumph Bonneville. And so the Bonnie legend was born. Naturally the Bonneville shook and rattled and leaked oil, but it was light and relatively quick. It wasn't, in fact, bad at all and if you were seventeen years old in the 1960s it was the bike to have. A bit like a Yamaha RD350 LC in the 1980s, though nowhere near as fast, or as fine-handling, or enduring. Or good looking, if we're honest.

The Brits were breaking world speed records and the industry bosses were awake and off the golf course long enough not only to read the memo telling of their team's success but also to maximise the achievement through the modern miracle of marketing. But on the other world platform for PR and popularity, race tracks, it wasn't going so well. Norton, who had been dominant before the war, could see the writing on the wall for its Manx racing models. These single-cylinder machines, built as 350cc and 500cc models, struggled against the Italian four-cylinder machines built by MV Agusta and Gilera, winning only two Grands Prix during the 1950s. Norton stopped building the Manx racers in 1962, by which time the Japanese had arrived and more trouble was on the way. As the 1960s progressed, Nortons became the favoured steeds only of club racers and international riders with no money. An ignominious state for a one-time legendary brand in racing.

But in 1967 there was a promising ripple of good news from the showrooms when Norton released a bike called the Commando. It was a very traditional bike: a 750cc parallel twin with a separate gearbox. A pre-unit twin, in other words, and about as modern as a candle. But it was a good bike and the world fell in love with it. Being a twin it shook like an Inuit nudist but the designers fitted it with a system called Isolastics: the engine and gearbox sat in a frame which was mounted to the main cycle frame via rubber bushes that absorbed vibration. This wasn't a magic pill and there were issues. Owners soon discovered that set-up was critical: if the bushes were too tight the whole lot vibrated terribly and if they were too loose the bike handled like a wheelbarrow full of cannonballs. But set up properly, the system was a success and the Commando very quickly achieved the sort of status that rings on down the decades.

Motor Cycle News, the weekly bible of British motorcycling, voted it their bike of the year for five years on the trot from 1968 to 1972. And that's astonishing when you think about it because in that period Honda launched its revolutionary CB750 and changed the world for ever.

Hot on the heels of Norton's 1967 success with the

Commando came yet more exciting news for the British motorcycle industry in 1968, this time from Triumph. The company launched a bike called the Trident. Like the Commando the Trident was hardly cutting edge. But it was a 750 with three cylinders. And that was exotic. Okay, the motor was a development of an engine that was designed in 1937 but it was, nevertheless, a good bike. Relatively smooth and with reasonable performance. Best of all, it could be tuned for racing. Ah yes, racing. The invisible force that drives humankind straight to the track with whatever machine it has just invented was still very much in action.

As soon as the Norton Commando of 1967 was launched, racers converted it for production racing and did well but then, in the early seventies, Norton picked up some sponsorship from fag company John Player. An unsung genius called Peter Williams, who was an engineer and racer, built a special frame that borrowed from contemporary F1 car technology. Williams was also the first person to fit alloy wheels to a bike. Peter Williams and Norton took their new smart-looking racer to the Isle of Man in 1973 and won the Formula 750 race against impressive opposition.

Meanwhile, similarly impressive things were going on at Triumph. And, amazingly, at BSA. The BSA Group owned Triumph and when Triumph launched the Trident, BSA launched its Rocket Three. The two bikes were essentially the same – what today we would call badge engineering – but against financial logic the bikes had their own frames. In 1971 Triumph/BSA did the same thing as Norton had done with its Commando and commissioned a frame especially for racing. In that year the company entered bikes in the prestigious Daytona 200. That was the big one, as far as sales were concerned. Win that race and American motorcyclists ran straight to their local dealer and bought the road-going version of your motorcycle. Amazingly, a BSA-engined bike was first, second and third.

Trouble was, things weren't going well at home. Japanese opposition was too tough in the showrooms, and there was the oil crisis – which was always going to be a problem if your bikes insisted on standing in a permanent pool of the black stuff, let alone actually burning the refined product and turning it into noise and speed. And there was always going to be a limit to how long you could sell bikes that were designed when Winston Churchill was a young man. Reality will have this habit of jumping in and waving its arms about to dispel all that lovely, dewy-eyed sentimentality and patriotism. They tried, though. It was becoming a struggle for survival and efforts had to be made to modernise. Norton treated the Commando to disc brakes front and back and an electric starter. The latter more for show and the benefit of the sales brochure because someone successfully starting a Commando by button was an event worthy of celebration with fireworks and the planting of a memorial oak. Triumph modernised the Trident, going a step further than Norton and producing the T160 model with new styling, disc brakes and electric starting that worked. Several times a year. The T160 was a handsome machine and so was the Commando, but the undeniable truth was that they looked like classics at a time when the birth of the superbike was around the corner.

You could write a book on the last years of the British motorcycle industry and its final death. People have. A chap called Bert Hopwood, whose career as a motorcycle engineer and designer had coincided with the heyday of the British bike industry, wrote the definitive obituary. We'll just skip through it because it's painful and it's all too obvious what was going to happen.

In 1973 the British government merged BSA/Triumph and Norton to form a company called Norton Villiers Triumph, or NVT for short. NVT was essentially the doggy bag of the British motorcycle industry, the last bits scooped up into one place. There were strikes, among them a famous workers' sit-in at the Meriden factory, which resulted in a workers' co-operative. By 1977 NVT was gone and Triumph was being run by the workers' co-op, which had bought the rights to the Triumph name. The last Commando was built in 1977 but Triumph continued with the Bonneville until 1983 when, despite an electric starter and refreshed styling, it was totally out of date. This was not finishing with a bang, but fizzling out.

So that's it then. The British motorcycle industry dead and buried. Actually, no. It would have been but for one very determined individual, a builder called John Bloor. In fact, John was more of a property developer type than a bricky – although he did train as a plasterer – but it's far more in keeping with the tone of the British bike industry and biking in general that we should think of him as a builder. I'm going to go the whole hog and think of him as a heroic bricky, striding on to the scene with the sun glinting off his hod and a confident, calming smile plastered across his genial but tough face. Now that is a motorcycling hero for you.

Bloor had bought the Triumph name in 1983 and reckoned

that it was possible to make a go of building Triumph motor-cycles again. Clearly somebody had left the lid off some noxious chemical at one of his building sites and it had affected his brain. That's certainly what the world thought, but the world was wrong. Bloor started slowly, concentrating on reliability and quality. He was not trying to build state-of-the-art super-bikes and take on the Japanese big four head on.

John ploughed in huge amounts of his own money and invested in up-to-date machinery and tooling and in 1990 the first bikes were launched at the Cologne motorcycle show. There were 750cc and 900cc three-cylinder machines and 1000cc and 1200cc four-cylinder ones. John and his team were not about to throw away all that misty-eyed love for the brand, so their new bikes carried traditional Triumph names like Trident and Daytona. Some bits of the old brand were thought best left behind, though, so the bikes were anything but old-fashioned. And in a significant departure from the Triumphs of old, the decision was taken that they should not vibrate or leak oil. They were quite staid compared to Japanese bikes, but Bloor didn't care. He just wanted them to work properly.

Those early 'Hinckley' Triumphs (Triumph is based in the Leicestershire town) made way for more exciting machines like the Speed Triple, 955i Daytona and Tiger adventure bikes. Within 20 years Bloor's Triumph motorcycle company was selling almost 50,000 bikes a year. Not just to patriotic types who wanted to buy British, not just to fans who liked the old Triumphs, but they were being bought by people who simply wanted a really good bike.

In 2003 the unthinkable happened: rider Jim Moodie won

the 600cc Junior TT riding a Triumph. The first win for the company in three decades. And it wasn't a flash-in-the-pan win. Triumph bikes are still winning out on the track. And in the showroom. It's a miracle.

THE GERMANS

When I was a teenager there were two things I laughed at – well, three if you include New Romantics. But the most important two covered between them the most significant anchor points of my life: cars and bikes. And those two objects of my cruel, mocking hilarity were Volvos and BMW bikes. Volvos I laughed at out of a fear reflex because they were all of them, each and every dreadful beige box, driven by myopic psychopaths intent on destroying me and my mates on our mopeds. The wardrobe-hauling, antique dealer's favourite, whether straining under the weight of a thirty-foot oak table on the roof or bulging with the detritus and hideous, sticky presence of a batch of eighteen children and their lifeless parents would inevitably sway about the road and threaten to crush us under a dump truck or else stop suddenly and for no reason – except perhaps heart attack or unexpected slippage of the pince-nez. In fact, the primary object of these oblong land-sharks was at all times to target and destroy all those of us with the temerity to take to the road on something built for fun, exhilaration and expression.

I may have overstated that a bit, but the common

conception among us was that Volvos were a bloody menace and you should keep away from them. Not sure how the Volvo drivers actually felt about us – I'd quite like to hear from one today – but then that sort of balanced view and empathy is exactly the sort of thing nature herself long since programmed out of the mind of the teenager for reasons best and only known to herself, so let's not question it.

And standing miserably alongside the Volvo as objects of derision were BMW bikes. They were big, they were slow, they were ugly, they had shaft drive transmissions, which aren't as sexy as a chain, and they made a funny sort of farting noise from their two miserable, ugly, flaccid, low-lying horizontal cylinders. They were ridden by posh people – judges, surgeons and thespians – who sat upright in the saddle like a vicar at a dinner table and scowled at us scruffy rascals in our torn jeans and outsized biker boots. Standing at the window of our family home in Ripon, North Yorkshire, one day in the mid-eighties I gazed out at the busy junction opposite and dreamed of the day coming soon when I could take to the road on a bike myself. A rack of BMW bikes had pulled up, waiting to cross the junction. They sat there, eight of them, with their stupid fairings and panniers and luggage and waterproof-clad riders and I hated their smug, cope-with-everything attitude. The end rider leaned their bike to one side as they sat there, perhaps to hook a gear ready to set off. They leaned too far, past the point where their single, shaking leg could hold the big machine and it went over. That bike hit the next one, which hit the next one and quickly the whole lot went down, felled as if by a missile. Oil, petrol, plastic fairings and shattered dignity cascaded across the damp tarmac and I struggled to know what face to pull. Bikes, real, valuable bikes had just been destroyed in front of me, through no fault of their own. Which was a tragedy. But they were BMWs. It was like watching toy rabbits being thrown into a blender: unsettling, but nowhere near as awful as if it had been real rabbits. Things would be different now. I have BMWs myself and they are a very, very different proposition today to what they were in my youth. And it hasn't all been marketing thanks to an actor and his mate clattering around the world on knobbly tyres and making a telly show about it.

To discover the roots of BMW's modern-day status, let's go back to a time way before a skinny, teenage Brummie watched in confusion through the window of his house in the North as eight BMWs laid down their lives due to the carelessness of the judge riding one of them. Let's go back

George Meier was the first 'foreigner' to win a TT race. He did it on a supercharged 500cc BMW in 1939. After a bit of a break he was back racing BMWs again in the late forties.

to before the Second World War and to a bloke called Georg Meier. A former police motorcyclist, Meier went to the 1939 Isle of Man TT as a member of the BMW works team. They took with them a machine called the Type 255 Kompressor. I'm not entirely fluent in German, but I can guess that Kompressor is compressor and that means supercharger. Germany led the world in engineering in virtually every area and its bikes were no different. This supercharged – yes, supercharged – 500cc bike had double overhead camshafts, two opposed cylinders and a shaft drive. It produced 60bhp and would do 140mph. The unthinkable happened: Georg Meier won the race and became the first non-British rider to win at the TT. The shock, horror and confusion must have rivalled the way I felt nearly half a century later as I looked out of my window in Ripon.

After the war the old supercharged bikes were wheeled out once more but BMWs never again made an impression in Grand Prix racing. Actually, that's not quite true. BMW engines did very well indeed, but in a less than impressive department of racing when it comes to generating sales based on a sexy image. They were virtually dominant in sidecar racing in the 1960s until Yamaha's awesome two-stroke TZ750 engine was fitted to sidecar rigs in the mid-1970s. Unfortunately, numerous victories in sidecar racing don't really help with boosting a company's sporting image. They might be more helpful to a picnic basket salesman.

You can't be as good at building machines as BMW without having at least some sort of sense of what's going on around you and, fair enough, the company wasn't entirely unaware of its boring image. In 1973 BMW produced a bike called the R90S. It came with a cockpit fairing as standard and had two-tone smoke paintwork. By BMW's standards it was pretty racy but compared to a Kawasaki Z1 it looked pretty tame. Looks are deceptive, though, because the first American superbike championship (held in 1976) was won by Brit Reg Pridmore riding an R90S. I've got an R90S in my collection. I mean, I don't ride it where anyone is likely to see me, but when I do, it's a revelation: that old engine may not be pretty but the punchy power is served up with a cheery determination and it can hunker down and hustle, even today. Though I wouldn't advise leaving the braking too late.

BMW followed the R90S with the R100RS in 1978. This bike had a full fairing that had been designed in a wind tunnel – the phrase 'wind tunnel' being as sexy in 1978 as 'laser star burst online hologram' testing might sound today. Its top speed of 125mph wasn't too shabby, but what was really impressive was that it could be ridden at 100mph all day long without tiring the rider in the slightest. Even I, only nine years old when it was launched, was impressed. I owned one a few years ago but it didn't stay for long. Still a bit boring, if I'm honest.

A BMW that I do still have is an R80 GS. It's the most important bike the company has ever made. GS stands for *Gelände/Straße*, which in English means off-road/road. Launched in 1980 it was the world's first big-capacity adventure bike. It was a new thing and as exciting as it could be, given the badge on the tank. But it had a much, much more important role to play further down the line as it grew and morphed into the R1150GS. This is the bike that took Ewan McGregor and Charley Boorman a long way round. If you go touring in Austria you will see that almost every bike is a GS and each one will be ridden by someone wearing leather dungarees. If you travel around any major European city you will see that many of the bikes there are examples of the BMW GS, too, but they are being ridden by accountants desperate to bring some rugged glamour to the business of tackling the mighty summits, valleys, deserts and jungles of, say, a commute from Fulham to Kensington.

Fantastic, BMW creates one of the most iconic bikes ever. With over 500,000 GSs sold, it is without question the most successful big bike ever made. But it isn't really a sexy machine (James May rides one). Still BMW had this image of being a bit sensible and staid.

There was nothing else for it. BMW had to build a superbike. Now this is a pretty risky strategy. After decades of building bikes for members of the House of Lords, could BMW actually build an exciting high-performance motorbike? Turns out that they could.

In 2009 BMW pulled the wraps off the S1000RR. Four cylinders, 1000cc and 180bhp at the back wheel. The world had to sit down to take it all in. It looked fantastic and was ballistically fast. It had loads of electronics on it to help you not fall off and several riding modes, including one for wet roads. These aids don't kill the fun, they just mean that you need to change underwear at normal intervals.

A superb roadgoing superbike is one thing, but to really earn credibility it has to go racing. And it turned out that the S1000RR was just as great a race bike as it was a road bike. On 31 May 2014 Northern Irish TT star Michael Dunlop won the superbike race at the Isle of Man on a BMW S1000RR. It was BMW's first win at the TT for 75 years, since George Meier won in 1939. BMW was, at long last, cool.

THE ITALIANS

Italians can't make a toast rack without spending months designing it. That's not an insult, far from it; it explains why nipping into town to buy a newspaper in Italy is an opportunity to show off your scooter, your loafers, your perfect trousers and perfect taste as you sip down a perfectly made coffee and meet your friends to form a natural centre spread straight from a style magazine. 'La Bella Figura' is a way of life for the Italians and it means, roughly, 'Cutting a Beautiful Figure'. It's part of the Italian culture: everything has to be beautiful right down to the last detail. And if you don't believe that, go to your local Ducati dealer. Or have a look in my garage. My Italian bike collection is getting out of hand. I'm up to 14 machines so far and I fear I'm nowhere near finished. My latest acquisition is a bog-standard Ducati 916. I wanted a bog standard one precisely because in its most basic form the 916 exhibits more Bella Figura somehow and is one of the most eye-wateringly beautiful bikes ever made. Its designer was the late Massimo Tamburini, the Michelangelo of motorcycle design. I bet he owned the world's most beautiful toast rack.

But it isn't just Ducati that make beautiful bikes. I've got Moto Guzzis, a Laverda and several Bimota in my collection and they're all wonderful. Sometimes they even start. Actually, they nearly always start, it's just that not everything works. Italians have had a reputation for dodgy electrics forever. Not entirely fair for them to be singled out because British bikes didn't have particularly good electrics either. But perhaps it's the scale of the disappointment that poured fuel on the flames of the reputation as it grew. Walking out in the rain to the shed to find your BSA Gold Star unwilling to fart into life because the condenser's on the blink only seems another inevitable detail in the picture. Strolling out in your hand-tooled loafers to find that your Ducati 916 has a failed headlight is like your dream date turning out to have terminal flatulence and is more likely to stick in your memory as something to tell your friends about.

There's one make of Italian bike that I don't have (it's only a matter of time) and that's an MV Agusta. It's somehow a fast-sounding name, and MV Agustas were fast. In the 1950s and 1960s they dominated Grand Prix racing. Even when the Japanese came along with their fine engineering tolerances and devotion to extensive development, MV Agusta kept on winning; taking thirty-eight world championships, the last one in the 500cc championship in 1974 with Brit Phil Read at the handlebars. By then, the frantic, two-stroke racing bike was well on its way and it's a miracle that the red MV Agustas with their old-fashioned four-stroke engines could still win.

Moto Guzzi and Ducati also have strong racing histories but they're virtually the opposite of each other. Moto Guzzi's great racing days were in the 1950s, the peak of which was their incredible V8-powered 'Otto', raced from 1957 to 1959. It revved to 12,000rpm and would do a smidgeon over 170mph. Ducati didn't have anything nearly as exotic as the V8 Moto Guzzi and instead concentrated on racing in classes for smaller bikes. And so it came as a bit of a shock when in 1972 Ducati entered a handful of its 750cc V-twin bikes against the big boys. The twin-cylinder engine was the work of Ducati's genius engineer Fabio Taglioni, who designed it and the 750GT that it went into in a matter of months in 1970. Much to everyone's amazement the Ducatis finished one-two at Imola with the winning bike ridden by Brit Paul Smart, who happened to be Barry Sheene's brother-in-law. A win at the prestigious Imola race meant sales on Monday and suddenly Ducati were on the map.

Six years later something even more amazing happened. Racing god Mike Hailwood, who until Valentino Rossi came along was probably the best motorcycle racer the world had ever seen, had changed to racing Formula One cars. Ironically, after surviving racing bikes in the 1960s, Hailwood spannered himself in a McLaren at the 1974 German GP. Not too badly, but he broke his leg and ankle and could no longer work a car's throttle pedal properly. Retired in New Zealand, Hailwood soon got bored and was tempted back to race on two wheels in the Isle of Man in 1978. He'd last raced there in 1967 and his fans were worried that he'd let himself down and spoil a great CV.

They were even more bothered when it was announced that Hailwood would be riding a Ducati. It'll be slow, blow up or both, was the general opinion. The bike had barely changed from that 1972 Imola-winning machine, apart from having grown to 900cc, but Hailwood did the impossible and won the Formula One TT. More sales.

At that 1978 TT race was a racer called George Fogarty. George's teenage son Carl was only 13 and no one would have imagined the massive role he would one day play in boosting Ducati's image. When the company launched its 916 road bike in 1994 it quite logically decided to enter the World Superbike Championship. Carl Fogarty, by now a professional racer himself, was one of the riders. Foggy was an inspired choice, hard, fast and never willing to give up, the Lancashire rider won four World Superbike titles for Ducati, a feat that without question sold a huge number of 916 road bikes for the company including one, a rare SPS 'Foggy Rep', to me. Although I'll be honest here and confess that somehow, for me, the basic version without the stickers, the loud exhausts and the terrifying engine mods captures more of that elusive 'Bella Figura'.

Meanwhile, what about the others? Just as Ducati was getting its teeth into racing, Moto Guzzi was closing the door. Instead it concentrated on building its iconic V-twin road bikes. These V-twins differed from those in Ducati and Harley-Davidsons in that the V was across the frame with a cylinder head in front of each of its rider's knees. They had something in common with Harley-Davidsons in that they make a rotovator feel sophisticated and describing one as 'agricultural' in the hearing of a farmer is likely to earn you a turnip lobbed at your head. The sporting 'Guzzi' model was the 850 Le Mans that was launched in 1976. And yes, I have got one. It's long, low, has a big bore kit on it and other engine mods of the period and riding it is like fighting a metal bear. The other iconic Guzzi was the California, a slow bike that was a rival to Harley-Davidson – a cruiser in other words. James May owns one of those.

Then there was Laverda. This Italian company was responsible for building a bike that kept 1970s bike enthusiasts
awake at night. It was called the Jota, a machine with a 1000cc
three-cylinder engine that sounded like a WW2 fighter. The
bike was said to do 140mph which in that decade made it the
fastest bike you could buy. It was a man's machine, heavy, big
and every control from throttle to clutch was designed to be
operated by a body builder. Or by someone who wanted to train
to be one. I haven't got one of those.

Sales and popularity have always risen and fallen for Italian
bike makers with appropriate flamboyance and passion. They
enjoy their time in the spotlight, soar to success and glory
for a moment and then make a total Horlicks of some aspect
or other of business, engineering or their relationship with
government, mafia or the press and fade for a bit only to come
strolling stylishly back into the spotlight as if they had never
left it. MV Agusta, with all its racing success, should have sold
zillions of road bikes. But that never happened. For a while
they made a four-cylinder 600cc bike that was more a touring
machine than sports bike, rather missing out on the chance
to cash in on their racing success. In the early 1970s the 750
S was launched. It looked fantastic but for some reason had
the old bike's shaft drive which weighed a tonne and stran-
gled the bike's performance. Throughout the early seventies
MV produced staggeringly expensive sports bikes that could
only be bought by millionaires. Then they had some financial
troubles and Cagiva bought them in 1991 and employed the
great Massimo Tamburini to design a bike – and you just have to
say that last bit out loud with an Italian accent to get a proper
insight into the world of the Italian motorcycle manufacturer.

His effort was the MV Agusta F4, possibly even more beautiful than the Ducati 916.

That's how it is with Italian bikes and Italian bike manufacturers. Temperamental, unpredictable, fiery, feisty and tempestuous. But often achingly beautiful and difficult to resist. In my case impossible to resist.

EVEL KNIEVEL

It is not difficult to get into the *Guinness World Records* book if you really want to. Just find something bizarre that nobody has done before or that nobody wants to do and then do it, usually lots of times or really quickly or while sitting in a bath. But while it's all well and good to display to the world at large your desperate craving for fame by eating the most Scotch eggs while watching a Lloyd Webber musical, it does carry more weight when the thing you're doing falls into one of two major categories: a) Difficult; b) Dangerous. Evel Knievel, the stuntman, chose to focus quite strongly on the latter category in his quest to be the best. It worked, though, and he holds the record for the largest number of bones broken in a lifetime. It's 433, by the way, a number that I can only imagine must include bones like that tiny one in your ear with the funny name that always stumps people in quizzes.

Born Robert Knievel in Butte, Montana, in 1938, Knievel's whole life was lived on the edge. Or, indeed, throwing himself off the edge. He was a successful insurance salesman but got the hump when the company wouldn't promote him to

The good news is that Knievel successfully jumped 13 double-decker buses in London's Wembley Stadium in May 1975. The bad news is that he crashed on the landing ramp and broke his hand and pelvis. He insisted on walking out of the stadium.

vice president after he'd only been there a few months, so he opened a Honda motorcycle dealership in Washington. Business can't have been that brisk because he found time to learn to wheelie a motorbike and to ride it standing on the saddle, taught by a local motocross rider.

Years before taking on the dealership, Knievel had, as a kid, seen a stunt show run by a bloke called Joie Chitwood and spent hours riding his bicycle round the suburban streets of Butte trying to recreate the stunts that had so impressed him.

I whiled away my childhood trying to be Evel Knievel on my own bicycle, jumping Action Man off a homemade ramp and falling off the back trying to wheelie. Strange, then, to think of Evel Knievel doing exactly the same. Of course, he couldn't really grow up wanting to be like Evel Knievel, but he did have a hero stuntman to admire and did exactly the same things in the pursuit of copying him as we did in our youth.

The bike business failed – not surprising really if the owner of it was to be found out the back being taught how to ride one of the motorcycles from the shop while standing on the saddle. I'm guessing some of his stock looked a bit scuffed by the time it got delivered to a customer. With the dealership closed down, Knievel decided he'd have a go at motorcycle stunt riding professionally. Being a born salesman helped; in America it was only ever half a step from salesman to showman and Knievel stepped right into the role, hiring a venue, writing press releases, setting up the show and selling tickets. A small crowd came and he popped a few wheelies and jumped his bike over a twenty-foot-long box containing rattlesnakes and two mountain lions. With this modest little event, he had set the scene for a globe-spanning career of daredevilry that would have kids and parents biting their lips and tightening their knuckles in fear and anticipation as their hero did it again. He further set the scene, and established the endlessly repeatable pattern of his life, by clipping the box of rattlesnakes with the back wheel of his bike. The only thing he did wrong, really, was to manage to land it safely; a mistake he would subsequently correct with pretty much every stunt he ever tried in the decade that followed.

Hungry for more – of pretty much everything it would

seem – Knievel decided that to make proper money he had to expand the show. He needed to include more performers and stunt co-ordinators, a veritable crowd of heroes and heroines stunting their little hearts out for the delight of America, allowing Knievel more time to concentrate on falling off bikes and breaking bones – that record wasn't going to break itself. He found a backer to supply bikes who wanted to call the show Evil Knievel and His Motorcycle Daredevils. Knievel didn't want to be thought of as a Hells Angels type so he persuaded his sponsor to let him change Evil to Evel. And so the legend started in earnest and A&E departments were put on a state of readiness.

The renamed show did its first performance in Indio, California, was a big success and the bookings came in. The next show was in Barstow, California, where Evel attempted a new stunt in which he jumped over a speeding motorcycle. Unfortunately he jumped too late and the other bike clouted him in the groin. It is to my eternal regret that I shall never get to hear the actual and precise noise he made at that moment. Once recovered, Evel decided that jumping over cars would be a great stunt and might entertain the audience better. A&E departments added extra shifts. In June the same year he tried jumping 12 cars and a cargo van. Now, science today tells us that a van is going to be higher than a car. Science has moved on a lot over the decades, so we can't be too harsh on Evel Knievel for not having the benefit of what we know now. Sure enough, though, science prevailed on the day and the back wheel of the bike clipped the van, giving Evel a not-to-be-missed opportunity to break an arm and several ribs. By summer 1967 Knievel had cleverly and rather imaginatively added concussion to the list and then in August he had more trouble with a van – I'm guessing it was that whole height mystery again – and broke his left wrist, right knee and two ribs.

You're getting the idea that perhaps Evel Knievel was in the wrong business? Well, it all depends on your definition of the business he was in. And anyway, you need to remember that this was pioneering stuff. First, the bikes were light years apart from today's motocross bikes that can perform 18 back-flips while the rider is pouring himself a G&T. Evel's first bikes were Nortons and then, into the 1970s, heavy old Harley-Davidson flat-trackers with not much power and crude suspension. Jumping a double-decker bus on an old Harley would be like jumping a bus on an old iron bedstead with an angry badger in it. And that science issue wasn't limited only to lack of hard scientific evidence concerning the height of vans; today's stunts can be simulated on computers, trajectories calculated and forces worked out. In Evel's day, a man with a cigarette in his mouth put a pencil in the air and grunted a speed from under his cap. Indeed, the only technology that Evel Knievel used was in the form of X-ray machines.

By the end of the 1960s Evel Knievel's imagination knew no bounds – though concussion can do that. He jumped the fountains at the famous Caesars Palace hotel in Las Vegas (landed short, broke pelvis, femur, hip, wrist and both ankles; Massive Score). He was working his way into the *Guinness Book of Records* and also amassing a considerable fortune along the way. But nothing prepared the public for his most famous stunt of all. On 8 September 1974 our star-spangled hero attempted to jump the Snake River Canyon in Idaho. For this amazing feat

Knievel had commissioned a steam-powered rocket machine christened the Skycycle X-2.

It was some occasion. TV crews were there and in his usual style Evel had cranked up the publicity machine to fever point. He was strapped in, the crowd quivered and stared and the Skycycle blasted off along the launch ramp. Unfortunately, its parachute deployed too early and the daring stuntist and his machine drifted back across the Snake River to end up on the same side as he had started from.

In 1975 the Evel Knievel circus arrived in the UK. The plan was for Evel to jump 13 buses. The event was to take place at Wembley stadium in front of 90,000 spectators. I was six years old at the time but fully aware of who Evel Knievel was. Not because I'd read about him in a newspaper or seen him on the telly, but because I owned an Evel Knievel Stunt Cycle toy. It came with a bike, a ramp and an Evel Knievel doll.

Evel Knievel is famous for his stunts and tally of broken bones, but he should also be known for virtually inventing merchandising. This was before Millennium Falcon models and Buzz Lightyear dolls. You could buy a Sindy doll in the 1960s but, well, who the hell wants one and, anyway, that was different because Sindy wasn't a real person. This was the first time you could buy a tiny plastic version of a real-life hero; in this instance a tiny plastic version of a man now reassembled in much the same way as the toy had been put together.

True to form, the Wembley jump didn't go well. The man with the pencil and no science had set the height and slope for the ramp and given Evel the speed he must hit to clear the 13 buses. It might be down, once again, to that troubling lack of science, or maybe Evel wasn't listening, but whatever, he didn't build up enough speed and clipped the last bus with his back wheel. He explained afterwards, from his hotel bed, that the bike's gearing was wrong. Yes, possibly, that could be the case, or it could be that an aged iron motorcycle with all the sprightly suspension, meagre power and aerodynamic proficiency of a road-grader is not the best tool on which to take to the skies; however briefly you plan on being up there. He said, after he'd got off the stretcher at Wembley with a crushed vertebra, that the crowd had seen his last ever jump. And they had.

His history suggests that although he was undoubtedly a prolific stuntman, he wasn't an especially good one. And it's true, the whole 'will he make it?' thing was rather redundant in Evel's case because you could be pretty much certain that he wouldn't. The question, in fact, would best be, 'which bones will he break?' Must've been like watching a roulette wheel. He certainly grasped the showmanship side of it, creating a global brand and building on every event like a PR pro of today. But he dropped the ball a bit there, too, when he took a baseball bat to his PR manager and rather tarnished his image with America's bright young things and their parents.

However, stuntmen aren't supposed to be ruthlessly efficient, socially adept and as media-sensitive as a new prime minister. We the public want to watch a slightly crazed egomaniac throw himself, or herself – with heroic disregard for the consequences – into an act that can only possibly result, to our frazzled minds as we watch, in their terrible downfall and injury. OK, it helps if from time to time they actually pull it off and amaze us by finishing their piece of daredevilry on their feet smiling and not always in the back of an ambulance screaming, but that's a minor detail. Evel was a motorcycle hero. It said so on the box of my Evel Knievel Stunt Cycle toy. Cantankerous, egotistical, unreliable, stubborn, vain and impossible: the perfect stuntman hero.

SHEENE

It's 1975 and motorcycling was thriving, but at the same time it was in serious trouble. It was an image thing. Founded as it was on the myth of lone outsiders – ruthless rebels lacking not only a cause but a sense of social responsibility and a rudimentary hygiene regime to boot – the whole thing was in danger of falling foul of the very things that defined it and gave it its sexiness and allure. Motorcycling needed some PR, it needed help with its image. It needed a poster boy. And boy did it get one.

Barry Sheene had everything that motorcycling could dream of to fix its image. For one thing, he was very much the real deal: he won the 500cc World Championship in 1976 and 1977 – the last British rider to do so. He was the last British rider to win a Grand Prix in the top class.

So he could ride. But he was also a biker; a proper biker. He was, I'm pretty sure, also the last professional motorcycle racer to drill a hole in the chin piece of his full face helmet so that he could have a last cigarette on the grid before the flag fell. He was almost certainly the last rider to feature in a television advertisement for aftershave.

Sheene was much more than Britain's last really successful motorbike racer: he changed the perception of biking in the eyes of the general public. And he started doing so from a hospital bed.

Sheene was Suzuki's star rider and in 1975 was packed off to race at Daytona in Florida. The rear tyre on his Suzuki burst at over 170mph and Sheene was thrown down the road and broke his left thigh, a leg, his right arm, half a dozen ribs and lost a lot of skin. A TV crew had been filming a documentary and caught the horrific accident and the terrible image of Barry lying crumpled on the tarmac. But the cameras also filmed him in his hospital bed, where he proclaimed that 'apart from a broken thigh, leg and arm he felt perfectly fine'.

His 'nah, that was nuthin' attitude stoked the flames of love for him in the hearts of bikers and wannabe bikers across the nation and the media quickly applied the bellows and intensified his allure. The footage of his crash and recovery not only made Bazza a hero overnight, it also caught the attention of model Stephanie McLean, who dumped her then husband and took up with Sheene to form a couple who were as glamorous and famous in the 1970s as Posh and Becks are today.

Sheene attracted and was attracted to all the right people, too. He was great mates with James Hunt, another world champion (in 1976), smoker, playboy and pin-up from an era when racing drivers didn't have managers and nutritionists or spend half of every day in the gym. Sheene and Hunt had other ways of keeping fit.

While bikers were still being banned from pubs that didn't like leather jackets, your grannie was thinking what a nice boy Barry Sheene was. Your grannie had heard of him because he was always in the papers and on the telly. He'd been on Michael Parkinson's chat show, too, with thespian and motor-cyclist Sir Ralph Richardson. Sir Ralph admired the flush-fitting petrol filler cap on the tank of Barry's Suzuki RG500 Grand Prix and how it meant that if you were to be propelled over the handlebars you wouldn't be leaving your wedding tackle on a protruding cap. Sheene was a superstar: he won at the highest level, smoked in his crash helmet, attracted super-models like wasps to jam, laughed off massive accidents and chatted on Parky with knighted thespians who talked openly to him about their wedding tackle. It was a dream.

Sheene achieved legendary status, dragging motor-cycling along with him for the ride. Comedy pop act The Barron Knights referenced Barry in one of their songs with the line, 'He was mean, he set off down the high street like Barry Sheene'. If you got caught speeding in a car in the seventies the copper would say, 'Who do you think you are, Stirling Moss?' If you were on a bike it would be Barry Sheene.

It couldn't last for ever: it would spoil the myth, the legend, the attitude if it did. Sheene had another huge accident at Silverstone in 1982. This one was not his fault either, as he came over a crest at 165mph and ran straight into a fallen machine. This was worse than the Daytona accident and nearly finished our hero for good. Two metal plates and 27 screws later Barry was fixed and back on a bike. The crash effectively finished his career and he retired from bike racing at the end of the 1984 season.

Well, not quite retired. The cheeky Cockney came back in the late nineties to race (and win) at the Goodwood Revival. In

2002, Sheene was diagnosed with cancer. Back at Goodwood that year, looking frail, he was met with a hero's reception. He died in March 2003. He'll never be forgotten by those who saw him race and by those who remember the days when you couldn't go into a pub wearing a leather jacket.

TT

The Modern TT: A breeding ground for heroes or a chance to prove we're stupid?

Modern life offers few opportunities for us as a species to prove that we're not stupid. High-visibility jackets, reversing hooters on trucks, signs warning that heights can be dangerous, ice may be slippery, wind can be blowy, water gets you wet, hot drinks might be hot and poison can be poisonous all play their part in turning us into zombies, wandering around with our massive, instinctive, wonderful, calculating brains switched into limp home mode, barely ever sparking into life with even a brief demonstration of our capacity and complexity.

There are rare occasions when we do get to prove we're not stupid: The German Autobahns – the ones with no speed limits – are not littered with fools who have thought that since they are allowed to go as fast as their car will go, they must do so immediately and drive into a bridge support. There are other rare examples like Pont De La Garde, a Roman aqueduct in France which, despite being very high – 160ft above a river bed in fact – has not been adorned with handrails and signs telling us that falling off will hurt. And yet the valley below is not littered with fools who died with a look of confusion on their face shortly after discovering that, no, fresh air will not support their feet. Because WE ARE NOT STUPID.

At the other end of the scale, though, is the modern TT which would seem, on the face of it, to be very much an opportunity for us to prove as a species that we are, in fact, stupid – with every year at least a few people dying on its 37 and a quarter miles. Some years, tragically more than a few. But if it does stand as an opportunity to prove we can be a bit stupid, it also stands as an opportunity to prove that we can be bloody brave.

We left the Isle of Man TT races in the early 1960s when Honda and the other Japanese bike companies fired a rocket into the cosy camp of British and continental makers by arriving at the TT and winning. And they kept at it. By the 1970s the Japanese were dominant at the TT with only an occasional upset, like in 1978 when the legendary rider Mike Hailwood came out of retirement and won on a Ducati. 'Mike the Bike' won everything racing had to offer in the 1960s, including a roomful of trophies at the TT.

By the time of his '78 comeback he'd not been to the Isle of Man for 11 years and in the meantime had raced in Formula One at the highest level until an accident at the Nürburgring mashed up his ankle and finished his car racing career. Against all odds, he won the Formula One TT on the Ducati. The next year normal service was resumed when Hailwood came back again and won the Senior race on a Suzuki.

From the late 1970s the TT races were dominated by a

bloke called Joey Dunlop. No one could understand his thick Ulster accent and no one could understand how he could be so fast on a motorbike around the terrifying TT circuit. Joey rode for Honda for most of his career and in his mind, that was his job: riding the bike. He didn't do the PR thing. Joey was his own man, fettled his own bikes and would never be seen wearing a tie let alone schmoozing the corporate world at a swanky restaurant in London. He entered his first TT race in 1977 and then proceeded to win a record 26 races over the next few decades. No one has won more. In 2000 he won his last big bike TT race at the age of 48 when most people thought he was too old to win again on a superbike.

Later that year Joey put his bikes in the back of his old van and travelled to Tallinn in Estonia as he had done for years to take part in local races held on public roads. He went there just for the fun of it, for the love of racing. In a wet 125cc race he slid off his Honda, hit a tree and was killed. At his funeral in his hometown of Ballymoney in Northern Ireland 50,000 people came to see him off.

Most people thought that Joey Dunlop's incredible record of 26 wins would never be beaten but a bricklayer from Morecombe in Lancashire thought differently. John McGuinness used to sneak on the ferry to the Isle of Man on his bicycle and go and watch the races, sneaking back home on the return ferry at the end of the day's racing. He set his heart on racing at the TT. And just as you might expect a bricklayer to be, John proved pretty stubborn and very, very determined. He made it to the TT and raced there for the first time in 1996, since when things have gone rather well for the down-to-earth bricky. To date McGuinness has won 23 races.

The experts, as they had done with Joey Dunlop, began to say that McGuinness had had his day at the TT after he had a couple of winless visits to the Island. Then in 2015 big John won the Senior race and raised the lap record in the process.

And that is worth a closer look. John McGuiness managed to get his Honda Fireblade superbike around the 37-and-three-quarter-mile course at an average speed of 132.701mph. That sounds fast, but the numbers don't tell the half of it. John McGuinness and hundreds of other lunatic racers start a TT race on the start line on the Glencrutchery Road in the town of Douglas. They start at 10-second intervals because a TT race is run against the clock, rather than with a mass start like a conventional race. By the time McGuinness reaches St Ninians crossroads not more than a few hundred metres from the start he is doing well over a 100mph. At the bottom of Bray Hill, which is lined by Victorian houses on each side, he will be doing 175mph. On parts of the circuit his bike will be hitting nearly 200mph.

In modern Grand Prix racing you sit so far from the track that you need a telescope to see what's going on. At the Isle of Man spectators sit on grass banks and watch bikes go past at 180mph no more than 5ft away. It's almost as terrifying watching the race as it would be taking part. Actually, no it isn't.

The bikes go through the quiet village of Kirkmichael at 175mph, through the town of Ramsey and then over the 'mountain' back to Douglas for another lap. McGuinness, his fellow professionals and the hundreds of amateurs who race at the Isle of Man for the sheer thrill of it, are modern-day gladiators. Possibly mad, but nevertheless supremely brave.

Warriors willing to risk everything for the thrill of speed, throwing down a challenge to a world wrapped in cotton wool. Heroes, all of them.

MOTOGP

If Sir Isaac Newton came back from the dead and watched a MotoGP race he would be intrigued, no doubt, but also confused. Yes, of course he would find himself wrestling with how his reincarnation aligned with his deeply considered views of a monotheistic God as the masterful Creator whose existence could not be denied in the face of the grandeur of all creation. But he would also, I suspect, spend a moment or two wondering what the hell good all his scientific and theological pondering had done when it appeared that his species had progressed no further than to stand around in huge numbers watching a small number of their own kind trying to die while packaged up in brightly coloured cow hides. But I'm pretty sure, too, that he would have scratched his head a bit and wondered if maybe his theories of gravity, motion and such were a bit flawed.

What he would see playing out before him would be a series of events that while sometimes appearing to conform with all his stuff about equal and opposite reactions and objects in a state of uniform momentum tending to remain in that state of uniform momentum unless an external force is applied, might just lead him to think that, yes, that's all well and good but things get rather more vague and woolly at the edges of that particular envelope. A MotoGP race is full of moments that have us, the spectators, wondering if it might all be down to witchcraft and black magic.

*   *   *

It wasn't always so. Motorcycle racers were always brave and heroic, they had to be, but they at least had the decency to observe the same laws of physics that bound those who had ridden in to watch them race. In the old days of motorcycle racing, right up until the early 1970s, riders sat in a perfectly symmetrical position on their machines. Bum squarely on the seat, the exact same amount of buttock overhanging right and left, legs carefully tucked in out of the slipstream and chin on the tank to maximise speed on the straights.

Then in the mid-1970s it all changed. Riders started hanging off their bikes in corners, so much so that their knees scraped along the ground. Barry Sheene was one of the early exponents of knee-down and it seriously upset the old school. Today's riders have special knee sliders – chunks of nylon velcroed to their leathers – but Bazzer and his mates just wound a couple of feet of 'gaffer tape' around their knee caps. It soon wore away but there was always the leather under-neath and then skin, so that you didn't wear your knee bone away. Actually, a lot of road riders wear knee sliders today, just for a Sunday morning scamper across a Cotswold or even a Monday morning commute into the city. It's an odd thing, but if you look closely at the nylon blobs velcroed to their knees you will see that the scrapes and scuffs across them have a uniform, even quality, almost as if applied earlier that day in the garage with an angle grinder rather than torn in haphazardly by abrasive tarmac through a tight corner. I don't know, it's just an odd visual phenomenon, I'm sure.

Today, real MotoGP racers lean their bikes through corners by as much as 64 degrees. That's crazy. They're leaned over so far that the riders' elbows scrape along the track. When my elbow hits the road it's generally a sign that I am in engaged in an especially vigorous and dynamic crash and the next things to touch down will be my crash helmet, hands and no claims policy.

Today's racers do things on motorbikes that really do appear to tweak at the nose hairs of the laws of physics. They slide them, braking, into corners and power slide them on the throttle, leaving black lines on the track. Again, like the elbow sliding, a sliding back wheel on my bike is generally an early stage in a process known as 'losing it', followed by another called 'binning it' and then another called 'hoping at first that your bike isn't as badly damaged as you are and then changing your mind and hoping that you're not as badly damaged as your bike'.

The MotoGP riders really are the cream of motorcycle racers and the very best of this select bunch are known as the 'Aliens', guys whose skills are out of this world. That is one cool nickname and one of the best of the Aliens has his own personal, even cooler nickname: 'The Doctor'. That's what most riders get to see written on the back of Valentino Rossi's leathers as they hang on for grim death and try to follow him around the track in the forlorn hope that an overtaking opportunity will somehow come their way; which, generally, it won't.

As any *Hitchhiker's Guide to the Galaxy* fan knows, 42 is the answer to the Ultimate Question of Life, The Universe and Everything. To motorcycle racing fans the number 46 means something equally important: it is the racing number of Valentino Rossi, who according to his old rival and ex-teammate Colin Edwards is the greatest rider of all time. Or, as the colourful Texan put it, 'The GOAT'.

Rossi was born in 1979, the son of GP rider Graziano Rossi. Graziano was reasonably successful but nothing like his talented son, who has won well over a hundred Grands Prix in all the different classes and also finds the time to be astonishingly talented on four wheels. He isn't, to my knowledge, scared of spiders, nor is he possessed of a funny lisp nor awkward looks. In fact, in yet more proof of the Lord's infinite capacity for being a bit uneven-handed when it comes to dishing out the finer qualities, Rossi is not just fast, successful and good-looking but he's also funny and cool.

Watch a typical post-race press conference in Formula One: three blokes in a row behind a table, two busy explaining why they hadn't won the race (wrong type of tyres, bad air in the tyres, track too hot/too cold/too grey) and a third bloke looking very miserable, who is the one who actually won the race. Contrast Rossi being interviewed after a race. He's grinning from ear to ear, proclaiming like an excited toddler after Santa has been that 'it was a great race, a terrific battle, fantastic fun, incredible'.

Only Rossi, after having won the 1997 British 125cc Grand Prix at Donington, would stand on the podium holding a bow and arrow and with a Robin Hood hat on his head. After one race, on the slowing down lap, Rossi pulled over, leant his bike against the barrier and disappeared into a Portaloo for a pee. Duly relieved, he jumped back on his bike and rode off to the pits. Cool, just so very, very damnably, impossibly cool.

But to be fair to all the other riders in MotoGP, and in super-bike racing, most motorcycle racers seem to be having a lot more fun than professional car racers. Perhaps the fun and humour comes from living permanently with the looming, grinning presence of extreme danger. Sure, the bikers race on modern circuits with lots of run-off and air-barriers instead of old-fashioned (and lethal) Armco and tyre barriers, but MotoGP bikes hit well over 200mph at some circuits and there's simply no getting round the fact that falling off at this speed, regardless of what you subsequently land on, hit or go through, is going to be quite sore. And then there's the dreaded highside.

Done well, the highside has many of the qualities needed in a motorcycling equivalent to the human cannonball. But don't let such a jolly image deceive you; the highside is something spoken about in hushed and dreaded tones among groups of bikers as might be the Jabberwock by, well, whoever spoke about Jabberwocks as a really, really dreadful thing. Basically this is what happens: the rear tyre slides, usually because the rider has opened the throttle too early or too much, and then suddenly grips. This would be a good thing, except that this sudden grip is just that; really, really sudden. As the tyre suddenly sticks to the floor it generates a huge force that stands the bike up and flings the rider out of the saddle and into the air. This is, of course, a bad thing and while I've never done it myself, some of those who have will tell you that the flying through the air bit is one of those moments that seems to unfurl independently of the normal laws governing time and the passage thereof. There's time, in fact, to contemplate many things but uppermost in the mind of the recently de-biked air traveller at this moment will always be the necessary and imminent business of landing. This generally goes quite badly, even if not interrupted by the arrival on the scene of a piece of street or track furniture such as a sharp-edged barrier or a signpost set in concrete. MotoGP riders bounce better than humans, it's one of their qualities as Aliens and they may actually have rubber skeletons, science is unsure, but even these guys regularly break bones in a highside. Presumably the leathers need cleaning in the seat area after one, too.

AUSSIES

If you want something fixed, ask an Australian or a New Zealander. Both countries are in the middle of nowhere and don't have their own indigenous bike industry. So if, fifty years ago, an Aussie or a Kiwi bought a Triumph Bonneville that had been shipped over and some bit snapped or fell off – which it would – they could either wait for months for a new bit to arrive from England (no DHL before 1969) or go into the shed and make the part themselves. No data exists, but it's likely that all households in Australia and NZ in the 1950s and '60s owned a lathe and spent a quarter of their annual income on Swarfega. Even today all forms of motor racing from Formula One to MotoGP have a disproportionate headcount of mechanics and engineers who come from down under. It's in their blood. Plus you often get to wear shorts if you're in a race team and they really like that.

But what about motorcycle riders? Australians are notoriously tough, wrestle with crocodiles and carry large knives. They bare their knees in town and they eat things cooked outside on metal grills covered in salmonella. Surely the perfect bike racer material? It was a heck of a journey from Australia to Britain in the fifties and sixties – still is as far as I'm concerned and I want to have a word with whoever decided to put the place so far away – so riders who wanted to give it a go in Europe had to be pretty determined. And determination is another Aussie trait, so not surprisingly quite a few gave it a go. More than one kangaroo sat on the dockside with tears welling in its big brown eyes – are they brown? Never looked – as yet another Aussie hero dusted off his shorts, pulled his corked hat down on his head and trudged manfully up the gangplank with his beer in hand to set sail for a bright future on two wheels across the other side of the world. And in some instances, it worked out. The first Australian to win a Grand Prix was a bloke called Ken Kavanagh from Melbourne. That's Ken for Kenrick, although his first name was Thomas. He's still with us, today a sprightly 92 years old.

Kavanagh first came over to Europe in 1951 but made his mark a year later when he won the Ulster Grand Prix and then, four years later in 1956, the Junior TT on the Isle of Man when it was still a round of the world championship. Having gone to the the trouble of making the 13,000-mile journey over here, Kavanagh thought he might as well give cars a go, so he bought himself a Maserati 250F and entered a couple of Grand Prix. He failed to qualify for Monaco and his engine blew up in Belgium. He probably fixed it himself with a spoon and a piece of wood. It was a bright start for the assault from Down Under on European racing, but not a dazzling one. There was much, much more to come, but it would take a while. Maybe it was the jetlag causing problems as they stepped from the boat...oh.

Around the same time another Melbourne rider called Keith Campbell caught the boat and came to Europe. Riding for the Italian Moto Guzzi team, Campbell won the 1957 350cc championship and became the first Australian world champion on two wheels. Sadly, Campbell was killed a year later riding a 500cc bike in the French Grand Prix at Cadours.

Several Australian riders followed in Kavanagh's and Campbell's wheel tracks but none rode themselves into the record books. And crucially, none won the premier 500cc class. And then Wayne Gardner arrived from a place called Wollongong in New South Wales. Gardner was one of those irritating people who are immediately good at something. Personally, I think this is a poor trait, failing to give proper respect to the dignified and essentially human process of learning something new, messing it up, learning it again, messing it up again and throwing in the towel in favour of trying something else and hoping nobody saw you cock up the thing you were trying to do before. Nevertheless and despite this failing in his character, young Wayne bought a second-hand Yamaha TZ250 race bike and came second in his first race. He tried a bit harder next time and won. No need to buy a boat ticket in the 1980s so Gardner flew to Europe where he raced a Kawasaki in the British superbike championship. His performance in that 1981 championship impressed Honda who gave him a job riding for them in the Formula One championship (a series for big four-stroke bikes).

Even more impressed, Honda Britain entered the Wollongong Whizz, as he was nicknamed – although given the Aussie predilection for abbreviating names he would more properly have been known to his countrymen as the 'Woowee'

– into some 500cc Grands Prix in 1983 and a full season in 1984. The 500cc two-stroke GP bikes of the 1980s were complete and utter animals, exuding a sense even at standstill that they were working quietly on some awful new way to kill you. In 1987 Gardner had the Honda tamed, well more or less, and became the first Australian 500cc champion. His victory got the Australian public revved up about motorcycle racing, so much so that in 1989 Australia held its first ever Grand Prix, at a circuit called Phillip Island. Gardner won it, which probably felt rather good. His teammate that year was another Australian called Michael Doohan. Again, Australians never use more letters than necessary – I think they believe them to be taxed – so Michael was known as Mick Doohan.

Doohan was well on his way to winning the 1992 World Championship until he had a massive crash practising for the Dutch Grand Prix at Assen in which he broke a leg. To bike racers a broken leg is like a broken finger nail to the rest of us and would not normally put a chap off. Unfortunately, there were medical complications with the repair to Doohan's busted right leg and at one point it was looking as though the saw would have to come out. But the saw stayed in the bag and although his leg would never be the same again, Doohan recovered enough to get back on his Honda; which is to say his leg was still hooked on and bent roughly the right way. He couldn't bend his right ankle enough to work the rear brake properly so had the mechanics fit a thumb brake. It seemed to work because Mick won the 1994 500cc championship. And the 1995 championship. And the one in 1996. And 1997. And 1998. In the 1997 season he won 12 out of 14 races, was second in two more and fell off in the last one. All this with a gammy leg. Only the great Giacomo Agostini and Valentino Rossi have won more premier class titles (proving that being Italian is even better than being Australian). Doohan retired in 1999 after crashing and breaking a leg in several places. Brave, but not crazy.

While Gardner was racing in Europe a star was born in Queensland. He was called Casey Stoner and he wasn't long out of his cot before he got onto a bike. Four years out of his cot to be exact, when, at the age of four, he entered a dirt track race for under 9s. It took him a while to learn how to win a race, and he was an elderly six years old before he did so. Then the winning didn't stop: 41 dirt and long track titles and 70 state titles before he was 14.

You can race in the UK at 14, so time for the Stoner family to get on a plane. They flew economy and lived economy. Stoner took part in the British 125cc Aprilia championship and lived for most of the time in a van with his dad. That was in 2000 and by 2006, having raced in the world 250cc, Stoner

A very young-looking Casey Stoner (it was the day before his twentieth birthday) during a press conference at Phillip Island, Australia, in 2005.

entered MotoGP with a privately run Honda. In his second race he was on pole but had a disappointing season with plenty of crashes and a best result of second in the Turkish Grand Prix.

The next year Stoner moved to Ducati and won the championship for the team with 10 wins. You'd have thought a long career lay ahead of him but Stoner is an interesting character. Moving to Honda he won the 2011 World Championship then, before the 2012 season had really got started, Stoner amazed his fans by announcing his retirement at only 26 years of age. Why? Because apart from having the traditional Aussie pluck and determination, he also had the characteristic dislike of bull. He found the politics in modern Grand Prix racing difficult to bear and said publicly that he wished he'd been around in the Wayne Gardner era when riders rode hard, partied hard and had fun. And as Stoner wisely decided, if you're not enjoying racing a bike at up to 200mph, should you be doing it and taking the risk?

SUMMING UP

There has been something missing from this short history of the motorcycle. And it's something frequently on the mind of the average motorcyclist and often for reasons other than the fact that another example has just pulled out without the driver checking their mirrors and has quite possibly in the process booked you and your bike a one-way ticket to the great breaker's yard in the sky. That thing is, of course, the car. There are those who divide the world into two distinct camps: Motorcyclists and Car Drivers. Indeed, there are those who view the world, life and their experience of it as being wholly about Motorcyclists versus Car Drivers. This narrow, medieval view, though, is not the right way of looking at it, any more than it is the right thing to divide the world into Drivers and Pedestrians. Because, quite apart from anything else, a lot of people are both. Take pedestrians: the lunatic pedestrian ambling across the road in front of your car in a headphone-swaddled blur as they text a picture of a funny swirl in a frothy coffee to their friends at yoga class is not, despite your protestations and raging at the time, 'a pedestrian' only; they might be walking from the office to their Nissan GT-R and thumbing through Nürburgring track times on their phone to see what lies ahead of them for their weekend away. Who knows? And likewise, the vacant-headed cretin who just pulled out in front of your bike in a van is a) more than likely not actively trying to kill you and b) quite possibly a biker at weekends which might be why he – or she – is working every hour their maker sends during the week in order to pay for tyres and maintenance on their immaculately restored Honda RC30.

So I don't subscribe to the 'either/or' view on the whole 'Bike or Car' thing. Like many kids I was desperate just to put myself in control of a vehicle that moved. Any vehicle. At the age of eight I clung for a while to a fantasy about owning a three-wheel car. The fantasy came from learning from a friend at school that it was actually legal to drive one at the age of sixteen as long as it didn't have a reverse gear. Sadly, somewhere during our earnest and excited conversation under the climbing frame we had suffered a fundamental misinterpretation of the law and my hopes were dashed a few weeks later when I blurted out my three-wheeled dreams to my father. It turned out to be far more complicated than my friend and I had thought and I zoned out from Dad's ramblings about different licences and insurances when it became clear that no, the drive of our suburban semi was not going to be graced by a purple Reliant Robin on mag alloys on the morning of my sixteenth birthday. And then, during another informal gathering of young motoring enthusiasts under the climbing frame at school it was declared by one of our number that we would, at fourteen, be allowed to drive a tractor on the road. Again, a frenzy of dreaming and scheming ensued. We looked up tractors – not on the internet, of course, but in the school library – and discovered that these humble, agricultural donkeys were far, far more exciting than ever we had realised and probably better than cars to drive anyway: they certainly had more levers. But those dreams were dashed against the stubborn rocks of the law, as well as those of practicality, fiscal reality and the fact that we lived in Birmingham, where a tractor is not considered suitable transport.

My subsequent discovery that I could legally ride a bike at sixteen, a full 365 days before I could get behind the wheel of anything as suddenly humdrum and unambitious as a car, triggered a reaction that took root in me down to a cellular level. My every waking thought was consumed with motorcycles and I held my breath until the morning of my sixteenth birthday, at which point I mounted my second-hand 50cc Honda and my life began.

So was my desire for a bike the product only of childish impatience? If I had discovered it was legal for a twelve-year-old to drive a rotavator on the road would I now be espousing in these pages the virtues and values of the powered earth-turner as an emancipating, life-enhancing force in its own right? No I would not. The motorcycle and the idea of owning and riding one took a hold of my heart, as it has those of so many others, precisely because there is something different about it, something that connects it more directly with our very being. Yes, it represents movement and, as I said at the beginning of this book, the ability to travel fast and far which brings with it the chance to dominate and flourish. But so, when you think about it, does a bus. It may be down to something as simple as size. The motorcycle is a handy sort of size; roughly the same size as we are, in fact. Maybe that is somehow significant to us, deep down in our inner psyche. A car is bigger; we sit in it and are surrounded by it: we are the operator within. A bike is fundamentally different. We sit on and not in it and we wrap ourselves around it: we embrace it. Maybe this triggers some clunky, archaic old synapse in the human brain connected with dominance, maybe it tickles another that signifies companionship and comfort, but the fact remains that riding a bike is closer to holding a bike than it is to something so banal and soulless as merely operating it like you might a car or a photocopier. And so a journey *on* a bike becomes a journey *with* a bike. Rider and bike travel together, work together to navigate tough territory, tight turns and unexpected events along the way. We experience the same weather as the bike, our body and the bike lean together and react to the same G-forces and if things go wrong are subjected to the same relentless tearing of tarmac or the sudden intervention of a tree. And we do all of this together, rider and machine, united as one.

A year after that first flush of motoring emancipation at sixteen I turned, like many, to cars. But it felt like a betrayal. Did driving a car at seventeen ever quite scratch the itch that the bike had at sixteen? Well yes, in many ways. I could take friends with me in my car, and together we could go on adventures to cities, to parties, to mountains and the sea. And I wasn't restricted to turning up in my ill-fitting leaky leathers and secondhand boots. In a car I could just hop in and hop out when I arrived, wearing the clothes I needed to wear for whatever I was doing when I got there. But I had bikes in my soul and within a year of passing my car test – and writing off my first car – I was hankering after a bigger bike. A Suzuki GP100 came along, and then a Honda and then another Honda and then a Yamaha, and then, oh and then a lifetime of hankering, desiring, saving, crashing, fixing, swapping, riding, fixing, crashing and riding and riding and riding …

I'm not alone …

There is fellowship among bikers, yes. We have looked at it briefly in this little book. And that fellowship is important, possibly because of its rarity in other parts of life and it is definitely enhanced by the visceral yet fleeting connection experienced between two bikers passing in opposite directions. And the fellowship of biking extends not just to other bikers, but to the bike itself. A late-night dash across dark, rain slashed hills is and always will be a special kind of private thrill. My sixteen-year-old mind would conjure up heavy metal images and I would ride faster lest the devil on my back leaned forward to take a bite. I still see that picture today sometimes and it makes me grin and roar into my crash helmet. And when my bike broke down, I didn't trudge off and abandon it by the side of the road. I took hold of it and pushed it and together we completed our journey through the rain and the wind, or if it was too far to push found a safe harbour where we could address what my heart and head felt and knew was really our problem; a problem shared. When my best friend crashed my Suzuki GP100 I wasn't cross with him, I was cross with myself. I had betrayed the bike, put it into the hands of someone who wasn't worthy and now the bike had paid the price.

Yes, crashing. I have crashed my bike. Indeed, I have crashed my bikes. I have been knocked off by cars, slid off on ice, misread grip on mud and gravel, turned too tight, too late, too fast and too slow; done some of the things that bikers do but never, never everything because there is too much to do in one lifetime. And no, I don't want to crash again. I never want to crash because that in itself is a betrayal of something I love. If I crash and spoil my life doing the thing I like doing best in my life, where will that leave me? And so I am careful, not reckless, because if I crash too hard I might not be able to carry on doing the thing I was doing when I crashed.

It's been a long-term relationship ...

It has been there with us during some of our wildest extremes. The motorcycle has shared and seen the best and worst of us. We have taken it to war, we have ridden it in marauding gangs, we have fought over it and stolen it. And it has provided us with a chance to demonstrate to the universe our technical ability, our imagination, creativity, our capacity for adventure and travel and our desire for communication. The bike you next see out on the road might be transporting an ugly thug with evil on his mind, or it might be transporting a new heart for someone whose children are desperate for them to live.

Has the motorcycle been responsible for creating any of the movements, moments, reactions and actions that have surrounded it since the moment of its birth over a century ago? No, of course not. Its invention and development have been an expression of something within us. We wanted the motorcycle so we made it happen. What we then did with it, what it has come to stand for and the changes it and we have been through together have been an expression of our personality as a species. I think we know this naturally and you can see it in the way that motorcycles are portrayed in films. If it's a film featuring cars, the car is very often the star. Whether it's the *Bullitt* Mustang, the *Dukes of Hazzard* Charger, Herbie, Christine the killer Plymouth Fury or Chitty Chitty Bang Bang it is the car that's the draw, the car that inspires us and which we lust after or fear. When a bike crops up in a movie it is more often the story of its rider, of their life and adventures. It is a social story. And that speaks to the bike's place in our lives. Whether it's a desperate loner, a drug-fuelled adventurer, a gang of reckless hooligans or a group of frustrated mid-lifers trying to live out their dreams before it's too late, the story is generally a human one and the bike is there as a supporting actor; a co-star, not a lone star.

...and it's not over

Right now, the bike makes more sense, possibly, than ever. Just the size of the thing when transporting one person to work through a busy city centre or urban area makes more sense than a car. And it's about more than physical practicality. Driving a car or travelling on a bus through a busy city can be a lonely experience. Ride a bike through any city in any country where the low cost and ready availability of two wheels make them the default mode of transport and your journey becomes a social event. As you draw up next to another rider wearing an open face helmet it's impossible not to smile or nod; you can see each other's eyes, see each other breathe and bear the same weather, wear the same day and you will chat as you wait for the lights. You'll arrive where you're going feeling as though you've been to a party.

There are people across the world who need to get mobile, just as there have always been. And just as has always been the case, mobility is often the answer to financial security, to enjoying as full a life as the place where you live will allow. Mobility, or the lack of it, is a huge factor in social equality and equality of opportunity. I have ridden with bikers in Uganda for whom a single-cylinder, Indian-made mount represents everything: a livelihood, a tool for communication, a goods hauler, an ambulance and even a hearse. A bike can be made more cheaply than a car, consumes fewer resources in its construction, costs less to ship around the world and uses less fossil fuel to move itself and its rider or riders – I have seen up to five on a bike in different countries. Once the problem of storing or creating the necessary electricity is resolved, the electric motorcycle will arrive in force and the next stage of the bike's evolution will take a huge leap forward.

Above all of this, all of it, far beyond any amount of philosophising and thinking about it, the answer is there, in my garage. And possibly in yours. Go out to it, pull on a helmet, slip on gloves while the engine warms, climb on and then just ride. Just ride. Because that's where it's at, right there.

ILLUSTRATION CREDITS

p.74 IWM/Getty

p.79 Mary Evans Picture Library

p.89 Pat Hathway/caviews.com

p.107 Manx iMuseum

p.112 Mortons Archive

p.117 Mortons Archive

p.124 Kawaski Heavy Industries

p.131 Daily Express/Hulton Archive/Getty

p.137 Peter Stackpole/The LIFE Picture Collection, Getty

p.148 Fratzer/Ullstein Bild/Getty

p.159 David Ashdown/Keystone/Getty

p.185 Cameron Spencer/Getty

PLATES

1 & 2 Henny Ray Abramds/AFP/Getty

3 Mortons Archive

4 & 5 Ellis O'Brien

6 Frank Monaco/Rex/Shutterstock

7 Columbi/The Kobal Collection

8 & 9 Bettmann/Getty

10 Mortons Archive

11 Takeyoshi Tanuma/The LIFE Picture Collection

12 Kawasaki Heavy Industries

13 & 14 Susuki Motor Corps

15 & 16 Mortons Archive

17 RacingOne/Getty

18 & 19 Ellis O'Brien

20 & 21 Mortons Archive

22 Robert Cianflone/Getty

23 Ellis O'Brien

24 Mortons Archive

25 Pbggalleries/Alamy

26 Don Morley/Getty

27 Andy Drysdale/Rex/Shutterstock

28 Bettman/Getty

29 Bob Thomas/Getty

30 Simon Miles/Getty
31 Getty
32 Lluis Gene/AFP/Getty
33 Mike Cooper/ALLSPORT
34 Mirco Lazzari gp/Getty

35 Ellis O'Brien